Identity Theft
The Cybercrime of the Millennium

by John Q. Newman

Loompanics Unlimited
Port Townsend, Washington

This book is sold for informational purposes only. Neither the author nor the publisher will be held accountable for the use or misuse of the information contained in this book.

Identity Theft: The Cybercrime of the Millennium
© 1999 by John Q. Newman

Published by:
Loompanics Unlimited
PO Box 1197
Port Townsend, WA 98368
Loompanics Unlimited is a division of Loompanics Enterprises, Inc.
1-360-385-2230
E-mail: loompanx@olympus.net
Web site: www.loompanics.com

Cover artwork by Linda Greer

ISBN 1-55950-195-2
Library of Congress Card Catalog 99-61780

CONTENTS

1

Introduction

Identity theft has become the hot crime. The thief steals the single most important possession anyone has: a basic sense of self — identity.

The concept of identity is an abstract concept that we reduce to real terms on a daily basis. Your identity is what makes you different than the next person, in fact, different from all other people. Your identity is what gives you uniqueness in the world, and also allows the world to know that it is dealing with you, a different individual than billions of other people.

To quantify an individual's identity we seek to use certain numerical and nonnumerical qualities of each individual. Ideally, these characteristics should not change, and when we single out enough of these qualities, we should be able to identify each individual.

One unique physical trait most people are familiar with is fingerprints. The chance of two people having the same fingerprints is so remote as to be statistically negligible. This is why police agencies fingerprint criminal suspects. Fingerprints, although fine for police purposes, cannot function as a day-to-day identifier for normal use.

Qualities that do not change over time are known as base identifiers. Base identifiers would be such items as birthdate, birthplace, sex, race, hair color, and eye color. Most identification documents such as drivers licenses and passports use a combination of these traits plus the individual's full name to create a unique identity for each person.

The chances of two people having the same full name, birthdate, race and sex is relatively remote, although it's possible as the number of people identified by a particular system increases. The uniqueness of these identifiers, in fact, is the basis of most identification systems, such as drivers license bureaus.

The computer looks for a match on all of the identifiers, and when no such match is made, a new file is created. We can add man-made identifiers to this list. In the United States, the most important man made identifier is the Social Security number.

The Social Security number functions as a base identifier because it should remain the same over an individual's lifetime. This is why the Social Security number has become such a requested item of information for all sorts of reasons that have nothing to do with income taxes or Social Security payments. Each Social Security number, in theory, should lead to records pertaining to only one person.

This is why most state motor vehicle departments require the number, as do credit bureaus, insurance companies, college registrars, banks, the military, and other agencies. Only a few of these uses are codified in law. Other uses have become common practice because people supply whatever information a form requests.

The nation's credit bureaus and insurance companies have long relied upon this. All of the credit bureaus use the individual's Social Security number as a file-retrieval tool, as we will see in later chapters. The growth of the Social Security number as a de facto national identity number means that no records with this number are very private. With just this number, your whole life history can be retrieved.

This is the one fact that the identity thief counts on. The other fact that he knows is that the vast computerization of private records held by government and non-governmental organizations allows records from one agency or business to be quickly matched up with records held somewhere else. In a matter of a few minutes an identity thief can put together a dossier on nearly any individual in America, even if all he had to start with was a name.

The fallout on victims of identity theft can be severe. In addition to having their credit ruined, victims can face more damaging consequences, such as being arrested for crimes they did not commit, having criminal records created in their name, or being made the subject of a lawsuit or paternity summons because someone else is using their identity.

We are all vulnerable to becoming victims of one of these computer grifters. We will see that the problem originates out of one of the basic tenets of a democracy: that public records must be made available to anyone who wishes to see them.

Chapter One
Information Everywhere

Information about us is collected from the time we are born until the day we die. In fact, a number of files about us continue to live in computers for years after our departure from this plane of existence. Some of these files are collected by government agencies, others are compiled by private sector establishments.

The statement, "Information is power," is even more true now in the age of the computer and the Internet. Information gives the critical edge in a variety of situations. Personal information databanks can be used to manipulate consumer behavior or swing public opinion for or against a particular policy.

Let's say a consumer is in the market for a new automobile. A few days earlier he received a solicitation from a local automobile dealer to come down and check out the latest sale prices on new cars. In the old days, this advertisement would have been mailed to many thousands of people without a lot of detailed forethought. Now, the recipient of this notice was probably specifically targeted to receive it based on a number of criteria.

The dealer may know that this is a person who tends to purchase a new automobile shortly after he has paid off the loan on his current car. The dealer may know that this person has a good credit rating and an income over $50,000 a year. The dealer might know this prospective customer is a family man with two young children.

A notice on the advertisement may tell the customer to present the card when coming in to receive a free gift or discount on vehicle service. A code on the notice will tell the prospective salesperson all about the prospect when he takes the ad to the back office and enters the code into the dealership computer.

The buying behavior of this consumer has been manipulated, and the customer does not even realize it. In the past, the consumer and the car dealer were on a more level playing field. The dealer had no idea of the customer's wants, needs, and financial capacity until the sales dance had been initiated by the customer. Now the dealer knows a tremendous amount about the customer before the game has even begun, and this shifts the odds greatly in favor of the dealership. Not only is the dealer more likely to make a sale, but the sale is much more likely to be made on terms much more favorable to the dealership than the customer.

How can the dealer learn so much about prospective customers? It is a direct result of the computerization and sale of personal information collected by private and government agencies. Little or no regulation controls what happens to this information, and it is freely sold to anyone who has the money to purchase it.

We provide personal data every time we fill out a form to receive some sort of service. Consider the vast number of private companies an individual must do business with simply to live. A partial list would include:

- landlord or property management company
- insurance company
- cable TV company
- telephone and utility company
- employer personnel department
- local schools for children

This is just a list of mandatory contacts that nearly all people must have to live. Now, add the following to the list:

- video-rental store
- newspaper and magazine subscriptions

- bank account records
- supermarket discount/check-cashing cards and clubs
- product warranty registration information
- other miscellaneous activities

All of these sources of information about an individual are unregulated. Before computerization, the personal data files private corporations collected were not worth much. Their utility was that they enabled a company to service its customers well. Without computers, personal information files could not easily be swapped or combined with files from other data gatherers.

Computerization changed all of that. As in the example of the automobile dealer, companies realized that the more they knew about existing or prospective customers, the more money they could earn by tailoring offers to meet the individual's specific need. But each type of business did not have all of the information in their records.

One company might have a customer's address and name, but not a birthdate. Another company might have the name and address of a customer's employer, but no other information. A powerful marketing juggernaut could be created by combining this data into a list with comprehensive information about each potential customer. Companies could also earn money by selling data to the marketing firms that create such lists.

In a later chapter we will examine in detail some of the players in this information free-for-all. But it is safe for any consumer to assume that whatever personal information they provide to a business is very likely to find its way to many other stops along the personal information highway.

One easy example to see this in action is to fill out a magazine subscription card in a totally made-up name. Choose the most outlandish name you can think of. Within a few weeks, you will begin to receive all sorts of mail in the name of this nonexistent person.

Private sector companies are but one side of the personal information equation. Government agencies at all levels are voracious compilers of personal information. What most of the public does not realize is that most information we furnish to government agencies is known as "public record" information. In the context of government personal information databanks, public record means that unless there is a court order or other legislation prohibiting its release, such information must be made available to any member of the public who wishes to see it.

Almost all individuals have some interaction with government records that are classified as public record. The following government information is considered to be public record in most states:

- voter registration files
- vehicle registration files
- drivers licensing files
- property tax and ownership files
- local civil and criminal court files
- bankruptcy court files
- incorporation records
- occupational licensing files
- military service records
- miscellaneous records

Regardless of the appearance of privacy when we make a transaction at a government department, such as the Department of Motor Vehicles, the actual records generated are usually public. This is one of the paradoxes of living in a free and open society.

One reason so many of our records are public is to avoid the type of abuse that can routinely happen in other nations. A friend of a powerful politician cannot be given a secret tax break on an expensive home without the public knowing about it.

Anyone can go find out the assessed value and property tax levied on any piece of property anywhere in the United States.

What the Founding Fathers had not foreseen was the development of the computer and the marshalling of all of this government-collected information for the enrichment of the private sector. One reason that driver, and vehicle licensing records are so widely available is because the auto insurance industry wants it that way. Quick and cheap access to these records allows them to prospect for profitable new customers and terminate bad drivers quickly.

Some states use the personal information that they collect as a source of additional revenue. Many states sell off their entire drivers license database in bulk to anyone who wishes to purchase it. The same is true of voter registration records in many states.

The increased traffic in personal information at both public and private sector agencies has caused the crime of identity theft to reach new heights. More and more people have access to your personal information, and anyone who is willing to purchase the data can do so. There is nothing to prevent one individual from using the personal data about a stranger for a legal purpose and another to use it for criminal reasons.

The computerization of numerous files has led to the creation of a new type of business called an information broker. An information broker will have on-line computer access to numerous databases, both public and private. Within a matter of minutes, he can create a dossier on almost anyone. Information brokers are one of the weak links in the system that allows even nominally protected records to be released to anyone who can pay the fee.

One main source of information brokers' data is the nation's credit bureaus. The credit bureaus are an excellent place to begin our study of identity theft because they compile more information on more Americans than any other private sector agency.

Chapter Two
Credit Bureaus — Partners in Identity Theft

You might be surprised to know that the biggest friend of the identity thief is the credit bureau. The credit bureaus would like us to believe otherwise, but we will see shortly that without access to their files, identity theft would be much more difficult to execute.

The credit bureaus are the nation's largest private collectors of detailed personal information. More than 150 million of the 260 million people living in the United States have files at one of the three main credit bureau networks. This means that nearly every adult in the nation has a file at one of these credit bureaus.

To understand how the bureaus operate, we need to understand the role they play in the credit-granting process, and how they accumulate their massive databases.

Credit bureaus, contrary to popular belief, do not actually grant credit. They provide information to credit grantors, such as banks and credit card companies, who then use the bureaus' data to determine if a loan should be made.

A credit report will contain the following information about an individual:

- full name
- birthdate
- Social Security number
- current address
- previous address
- employer name

- job title or position
- list of all credit accounts and payment status
- public record items
- most recent inquiries in the file

How do the bureaus get their information? The credit bureau industry underwent major changes over the last twenty-five years. Credit bureaus began as local operations, set up to serve local merchants who wanted to offer customers accounts.

Back then, the merchants performed their own credit screening. They would call a customer's employer, bank and other references listed on the application. Only after all of these references had been checked satisfactorily would they call the local credit bureau.

In those days, local credit bureaus were primarily a repository of information on people who did not pay their bills. If a merchant had to write off an account because of customer nonpayment, he would report the details of this to the local credit bureau. If this individual subsequently attempted to obtain credit at another local merchant, the application would be denied when the new merchant contacted the bureau.

Back then, most people were not in the files of the local credit bureau, and credit bureau databases were a source of negative information on a relatively small number of citizens.

Large data-processing firms realized that the fragmented credit bureau industry was ripe for consolidation and change. Now, almost all "local" credit bureaus are actually branches or affiliates of the three main credit bureaus. The three main bureaus are Experian, Trans Union and Equifax. How and why did this consolidation occur?

The large bureaus made the point to local operations that by affiliating with them they could obtain more information about each credit applicant, hence making their product more valuable to their customers, the credit grantors.

A local bureau would not know if a particular customer who was now living in Seattle, Washington, had left behind a trail of unpaid bills in Atlanta, Georgia. An affiliation agreement with the big bureaus would eliminate that gap. In return for sharing their files with the big bureau, the local bureau would gain access to the files of the large bureau. This would allow the local bureau to advertise that it could perform "nationwide" credit checks on local credit applicants.

Simply controlling the local bureaus was not enough for the credit bureau giants. They wanted to be able to increase the number of credit reports sold to credit grantors. And this is the central business of any credit bureau — selling as many credit reports as possible. Each credit report a bureau supplies to a credit grantor earns the credit bureau money.

One way to dramatically increase the number of credit reports sold was to turn the credit bureau into an information repository on all consumers. Instead of credit grantors just reporting the names of customers whose debts were written off, why not report the payment history of all customers, good and bad?

This is exactly what happened. Nearly all credit grantors report to the bureau monthly on the status of all of their customer accounts. The following information is usually reported on each account:

- account number
- account balance
- type of account
- credit limit and current balance
- minimum payment due
- account opening date
- payment rating from 0 to 9

This now means that a credit report shows a detailed snapshot of a customer's current indebtedness and a view of how the customer pays his bills over time. The next step was to increase the number of information sources the credit bureaus used to develop information on individuals in their files.

One such method was to mine public records for any matches, and then add these to the customer's credit report. Credit bureaus regularly receive reports from the federal bankruptcy courts and local courts on all bankruptcy filings and civil judgments or lawsuits.

If a person was being sued, or filed for bankruptcy, this information would probably find its way into the credit report. The credit bureaus could now truly say that they have everyone's name and number.

This allowed them to make another sales pitch to credit grantors, and increase once again the number of credit reports sold. Because the credit bureaus had become such a comprehensive source of information on all adults, most credit grantors could cease performing any credit screening or checking in-house, and instead rely only on the information the credit bureau supplied.

The credit grantor could save money because staff could be fired from the credit department, and credit decisions would be much faster. The computer would even allow for credit to be granted instantly for those who qualify. This is the current situation. Most creditors only rely on the credit report information when approving credit cards, automobile loans, and similar credit extensions.

From a privacy standpoint, all of this was fine, until the late 1980s. A business had to have a permissible purpose under the Federal Fair Credit Reporting Act to access a consumer's credit report. No information could be released from the credit report otherwise.

The Federal Trade Commission changed all of this. A Bush Administration political appointee agreed to remove the privacy protection from all parts of the credit report except information about the actual account. The rest of the information on the credit report, known in the industry as "header" information, could now be freely sold to anyone who wished to purchase it.

The credit bureaus wanted this change because they could see an entirely new market for these header or identification reports. The new customer list would consist of skip-tracing companies, private investigators, attorneys, repo men, information brokers, alumni associations looking for lost individuals, and other agencies.

This is how the credit bureaus became partners in identity theft. No reason is needed to purchase one of these header reports, and the credit bureaus isolated themselves even further by selling these reports almost exclusively via third-party information brokers.

There are two types of header reports. The first one is known as the Social Security trace report. To run this report, all one must do is supply the Social Security number. The number will be matched against all of the files in the credit bureau database and the following information will be returned:

- full name of everyone using this Social Security number
- current and previous address of these individuals
- birthdates of these individuals
- employers of these individuals
- telephone numbers on some reports

The second report is known as a national identifier or address-lookup report. The only items needed to run this type of report are the person's name, and an address from within the last seven years. The output of this search will be the individual's current and previous address and also the Social Security number.

These searches typically cost less than $40. In their greed to make more money, the credit bureaus have become the partner of the identity thief. Identity thieves purchase these information reports from information brokers to do their dirty work. In an upcoming chapter we will look at the wild, unregulated world of the information broker.

First we need to first look at what information from the government the information broker can access. We will see that, in many cases, the government is almost as willing a helper to the identity thief as the credit bureaus are.

Chapter Three
Government Data and Identity Theft

An Oregon man is pulled over for a routine traffic stop in Portland. After the police officer runs his name and drivers license number through the wanted person's file on his computer, he returns and arrests the driver on an outstanding felony warrant issued in a southern state.

The driver protests to the police, arguing that they have the wrong man. The Portland police, having heard this story a million times, tell the hapless driver that he will have to take the matter up with the other state after he is returned there to face the charges.

The driver does not give up. He hires a lawyer, and his employer is able to verify that he was at work on the day and time that the crime occurred in the far-off state. Finally, a fingerprint check confirms that the man arrested in the southern state and the Portland motorist are not the same person. He is immediately released, but his troubles are far from over.

This man was the victim of identity theft. Somehow, another person was able to learn the victim's drivers license number, its expiration and issue dates, his birthdate, and other pertinent data. With this information he could easily purchase a false license in the victim's name — a false license that would pass when a police officer checked it with his computer. How could the identity thief get this information? The government itself might have provided the information.

Earlier we mentioned that not only private businesses, but also state, local, and federal government agencies traffic the personal information they receive to service members of the public.

The concept that information provided to a government agency would only be used for the purpose for which it was given was eroded during the 1980s. Ronald Reagan used the example of the welfare mother who collected more than $100,000 a year in benefits by claiming numerous nonexistent children as dependents as a way to launch a new program. This program was known as data matching, and it was the beginning of the end of privacy in personal information provided to government agencies.

Data matching involves the comparison of two sets of information to look for common items. Data matching now occurs with numerous government files. Until computerization, data matching would have been very difficult, if not impossible.

For example, all newly hired federal employees have their personal identifiers checked against a list of people who are registered with the Selective Service System, wanted for overdue child support payments, or are delinquent on student loans. Some states routinely run their drivers license file database against those who owe overdue child support, and cancel the licenses of anyone who shows up on the list. The Internal Revenue Service will intercept tax refunds due those who owe overdue child support and certain other obligations.

Regardless of whether one agrees with the social purposes associated with data matching, one thing is true: It has meant the near-complete erosion of privacy with regard to personal information provided to almost any government agency.

The second destroyer of personal privacy and helper of the identity thief has been the computerization of public records. Public records do not threaten individual privacy when they are kept in dusty files at the county recorder's office or courthouse. These records do threaten privacy when they are placed in computer files and then sold by government agencies to whomever wishes to purchase them.

Consider drivers licensing records maintained by state motor vehicle departments. The drivers license is the one identity document most Americans obtain during their lifetime. Most states classify drivers licensing files as public record documents, and for a few dollars anyone can buy the driving record of anyone else.

The driving record will usually contain the following information about the individual:

• full name of driver

• birthdate

• license number

• issue date and expiration date

• status of license

• driver address

• test scores, points against license

• details of previous licenses

Many states allow anyone to purchase the entire driver database on CD-ROM. When the driver database is sold this way, the identity thief will also get a photograph of each license as well as the tabular data.

It is very probable the Oregon man who was victimized was hit by an identity thief who purchased the entire database of Oregon drivers. Once he had the database in his possession he merely had to search until he found an Oregon driver who was about his same height, weight, hair, and eye color. A fake license could then be purchased with this information. The fake licenses available today are of such high quality that they often cannot be detected, even by trained police officers. This method of identity theft, which we will discuss in more detail later, is known as "ghosting."

Drivers license files are not the only public records that state and local governments sell to outside parties. In some states, workers' compensation files are public record documents. Anyone who has ever drawn workers' compensation benefits because of a job-related injury can have their personal details sold to anyone. These files can contain very sensitive information, such as injury descriptions and details of treatment.

Anyone who owns a home or other real property can have very detailed financial information about themselves sold to the public. A number of firms compile this data. Two of the most popular are Dataquick and TRW Redi Property Services. The average homeowner must obtain a mortgage to purchase a house. The contract includes a lot of information about the property purchased and the terms and conditions of the mortgage.

When someone purchases a house with a mortgage, the lender files a lien against the property at the local courthouse. This document validates the lender's interest in the property and sets out the terms of the mortgage. Between this document and the files of the county tax office, the following information can be learned:

- name of mortgage lender
- exact address of property
- description of property
- sale amount of property
- mortgage terms and conditions
- name of legal owners
- address for tax bills
- property tax assessment
- any liens against the property

Property records like these are commonly used by identity thieves to locate high-income individuals. These records can also be used by identity thieves to obtain a second mortgage on the victim's house without their knowledge.

Voter registration records are another wide-open source of information for the identity thief. Voter registration records must be available for public inspection because democracy depends on voting lists being public documents. Once again, computerization and sale to third parties has now turned this into a useful source of personal data for identity thieves.

About twenty states have consolidated local county-maintained voter registration files into one statewide database. These statewide databases are commonly sold to information brokers en masse, who then resell individual searches to the general public. These databases can also be purchased by the public directly.

A typical voter registration file will contain the following information:

- voter name
- voter address
- voter birthdate
- Social Security number (in some states)
- sex
- voter telephone number (in some states)

Just driving someplace in your car can make you the victim of an identity thief. Most states sell vehicle registration information for a nominal fee. All that is needed to access such information is a license plate number or vehicle serial number. In a later chapter we will see how some identity thieves use this information source as a starting point when beginning an identity theft operation.

Chapter Four
The Wild World of the Information Broker

A key player in the identity theft game is the information broker. The information broker acts as the crucial link between numerous private and public databases and the identity thief. By using an information broker, the identity thief leaves no traces of his actions, and can obtain even privacy-protected information illegally with little or no trouble.

Information brokers emerged decades ago as firms that primarily serviced private investigators, attorneys, and banks. They would have contacts at different government agencies that could locate information and find copies of documents. If a private investigator needed a copy of a divorce decree from a neighboring state, his information broker would contact someone who could obtain the necessary information. In the main, these firms did not deal with the public.

The computerization of personal information records changed the business dramatically. No longer did an information broker have to physically send someone to retrieve a copy or extract of a record. It could all be done in the office via computer and modem. Most large information brokers can now access the following information databases for their clients:

- driver license records
- vehicle registration records
- criminal record information
- credit bureau header information
- complete credit reports
- voter registration information

- property ownership records
- occupational licensing information

This is but a partial listing of the information that brokers can access. The brokerage industry has split itself into two parts. Some more professional information brokers have decided to continue to restrict the sale of their information to their clientele of the past — "legitimate" clients such as private investigators, and lawyers.

These brokers will frequently require new clients to fill out lengthy applications, and will verify the credentials and references of those it supplies data to. These brokers do not want their firms to become the proxies of identity thieves or just plain nosy individuals.

The second type of information broker sells his wares to anyone who wishes to purchase them. No checking is done on the credentials of any customer. Many of these brokers advertise on the Internet and specifically offer a package deal of discounted services that will allow someone to purchase an entire dossier on an unknowing victim. These are the firms that identity thieves prefer doing business with. One such firm can be found on the Internet at http:\\www.docusearch.com.

Information brokers can also allow identity thieves to access full credit reports on unsuspecting victims. How can this be? Loopholes in the law allow it to happen on a daily basis.

Credit bureau information is available either directly from the bureau or via a third party vendor, such as an information broker. Most banks and other large direct lenders maintain direct access to the credit bureaus.

These firms have computer terminals that are directly linked to the credit bureau mainframe. Each direct access client is assigned a subscriber code by the bureau concerned, and the employees with bureau access are assigned individual passwords.

To become a direct subscriber, a business must pass a number of screening checks by the credit bureau. The credit bureau will require documentation showing how long the business has been in operation, the names and backgrounds of its owners, and current trade references that they can verify. The bureau may also require photographs of the outside and interior of the business, or may send a representative to physically check on the premises.

Every credit report that a direct subscriber orders will have the subscriber's name and identification number recorded in the inquiry section of the credit report. This is important, because it allows the identity theft victim to know exactly who ordered the credit report.

Because of these safeguards, direct subscribers account for very few of the identity theft cases. When a direct subscriber is implicated in an identity theft case, it is usually a wayward employee with bureau access who was tapping into the database.

Indirect access via an information broker is an entirely different matter. Once again, we need to make some distinctions between the two types of brokers. Very little identity theft can be traced to the information brokers who sell only to established businesses having a need for credit reports.

Why would a business choose to go through a broker to access credit reports instead of becoming a direct subscriber? If a business purchases only a few credit reports, it is cheaper to go via an information broker than to become a direct bureau subscriber.

Many information brokers will allow customers to access full credit reports with very little formality. A number of brokers require only a signed statement from the customer that they will access credit reports only when they have authority to do so under the Fair Credit Reporting Act. This signed statement is enough to protect the information broker from lawsuits if the customer is later caught misusing credit reports for identity theft purposes.

Identity thieves enjoy having access to full credit reports instead of just header information because it allows them to expand the size and scope of the identity thefts and other frauds they can commit.

A full credit report will detail the entire financial and credit history of the potential victim. With this additional information, the identity thief can take over existing bank accounts, loot pension funds, and wreak other havoc on the victim. The credit report will contain additional confidential information that financial companies use to verify the identity of an individual.

Full credit reports will also contain what is known as a credit risk score. This information, which is not even released on credit reports given to individuals, allows an identity thief to know in an instant if the potential victim is a good mark for identity theft.

Identity thieves are interested in people with good financial and credit records. Although header data can provide the identity thief with enough personal identifiers to steal a victim's identity, it does not guarantee that the potential victim has good credit.

The identity thief's motivation is financial gain, and he is only interested in stealing the identities of those people from whom he can extract a profit. Credit bureau risk scores provide a quick way to locate the most promising prospects.

Risk scores started to be added to consumer credit reports in the mid-1990s. A risk score eliminates the need for a creditor to review the entire credit report. Many credit grantors now only request the risk score from the credit bureau when opening new accounts.

The risk score attempts to reduce the mathematical odds that a given borrower is likely to default on his obligations or declare bankruptcy. The model that the risk score is derived from is based upon looking at thousands of individuals over the years who were granted credit, and finding the common trends that predict which of those people went bankrupt or defaulted later on. The risk score model will examine such items as how many credit lines the individual has, the total amount of debt accumulated, payment history, and the rate at which credit lines are exhausted. All of this is boiled down into a number.

A number of different risk scoring models are in use. One of the more popular ones rates a customer between 300 and 800. A 300 score means the individual is almost one hundred percent certain to default, and an 800 score means that the borrower shows almost no chance of defaulting on an obligation. The higher the score, the more desirable the person is as a customer.

Clearly, for the identity thief, access to full credit report information and risk scores allows him to quickly assemble a portfolio of individuals who are ripe to be victimized. The detailed financial data provided on a full credit report also makes the identity thief's dirty work safer.

With the full financial history of the victim at hand, the identity thief can avoid certain mistakes. He will not accidentally apply for a new credit card account from a bank where the victim already has an account. He can also decide what type of identity theft he wishes to execute on the victim. In an upcoming chapter we will see that there are many different types of identity theft that can be carried out. Some are done by individuals, others are planned by organized crime rings who specialize in identity theft.

One recent case of organized identity theft involved a ring that was headed by a Nigerian national living illegally in the United States. He bragged to his friends back home in Nigeria that he could acquire almost any item they desired. When he was arrested, it was estimated he had acquired more than 8 million dollars in cash and goods, which were then resold to his customers in the United States and Nigeria for a tidy profit.

As we have seen, the unregulated world of the information broker is a key link in the growing crime of identity theft. Information brokers allow identity thieves one-stop shopping in acquiring the personal details of their victims. An information broker can access credit, motor vehicle, voter and property ownership records on anyone very quickly for a reasonable price.

Chapter Five
The Fake ID Seller —
Another Part of
the Identity Theft Game

Identity thieves need to obtain identification in the names of their victims. Most types of identity theft will involve false identification being used by the criminal at some point in the game. High quality false identification is available from a number of different sources, despite attempts by the federal government to tighten the laws on mail-order identity documents.

Fifteen years ago the federal government decided to crack down on the sellers of fake ID. A law was passed making it a federal crime to manufacture and sell identification documents, unless certain requirements were met.

The federal law requires that the disclaimer "not a government document" be printed on any privately made identity document that purports itself to be a birth certificate, ID card, drivers license, etc. The loophole of the law is that as long as the fake ID seller agrees to put this disclaimer on the document, he can produce whatever type of fake ID he wants to.

One can now purchase exact replicas of state issued birth certificates and drivers licenses, all of course, with the disclaimer. The problem with the law, (or benefit, from the identity thief's perspective), is that it did not account for the rapid growth of computer power over the intervening years, or for human ingenuity.

The law does not specify that the "not a government document" disclaimer be printed in indelible ink, or where on the document it must appear. One seller of high quality fake drivers licenses prints the disclaimer so that it can be conveniently removed with a paper cutter without affecting the rest of the document. A seller of birth certificates prints the disclaimer in ink that is erasable with a regular pencil eraser. Presumably, the purchaser of the document knows what to do.

Other fake identity documents can be sold with no disclaimer, provided that they do not contain a birthdate. Many different forms of identity documents are available, from student and employee identification cards to cards that identify the possessor as a photographer or bounty hunter.

The Internet has created an additional source of fake identity documents. Numerous sellers of fake identity documents have set up shop. Some of these businesses are not subject to the federal law; others operate openly in defiance of it. Because the Internet knows no national boundaries, many of these firms operate quite legally by shipping their product from outside of the United States. Others will have all payments sent to an address outside of the United States. The actual documents are produced at a secret location in the United States and mailed to the buyer. Identity thieves are big customers of the Internet fake ID shops.

The Internet fake ID sellers will frequently offer exact duplicates of the current issue drivers licenses and state identification cards. Their wares will not have the disclaimer on them.

The final type of fake ID seller that identity thieves will patronize is the document replacement service. These companies will replace any document the owner claims to have lost. These companies specialize in such items as university degrees, birth certificates, award certificates, military discharge certificates, etc. The long-term identity thief is likely to be their biggest patron.

Chapter Six
Other Information Sources for Identity Thieves

We have examined some of the main information sources that identity thieves use to compile personal dossiers on their victims. But credit bureau files, driving records, voter registration data and license plate information are not the only places where identity thieves accumulate the grist for their crimes.

In fact, these information sources are tapped only after potential targets have been identified. This is because all of the above listed information sources will cost the identity thief or organized gang money to obtain via an information broker.

In addition, these information sources, although valuable, do not provide all of the additional information an identity thief will want to have when taking over the victim's identity. Let's look at some examples of past identity thefts to discover what other information sources identity thieves will typically consult.

One ring of identity thieves operated in the Pacific Northwest for a number of years in the mid 1990s. This ring specialized in stealing the identities of university professors. Numerous faculty members at a leading university in Washington State had their identities stolen before this ring stopped operating in the late 1990s.

How had the identity thieves singled out these individuals? University professors, as a group, possess many of the traits identity thieves look for in a victim. They are paid well, have good job security, and can be very profitable to rip off. A person making an inquiry about a university professor does not arouse much interest.

What made these people vulnerable was that their names, work titles, employer, and academic background were all public record information. All the identity thieves needed to do was consult the current edition of the university catalog to learn this about the victims.

Many universities make it very easy to learn how long someone has worked there by providing a central number to call to verify the employment status of any faculty or staff member. By just reading the catalog and making one telephone call the identity thieves were able to learn the following about each of their intended victims:

- full name of professor
- job title
- years at the university
- previous employer
- work telephone number
- academic background
- salary range

The home address and telephone number could be learned by then consulting the local telephone directory for a listing in the professor's name. Once all of this information had been compiled, the only other data needed for identity theft is the Social Security number and birthdate. This could be purchased from an information broker for less than $20.

There is even a national directory of faculty members at all U.S. universities and colleges that is available at most larger public libraries.

We can broaden this information source to include all employment-related publications that provide information on people who work in a particular industry. These directories can provide the first level of screening of victims for identity thieves.

One couple used a *Who's Who* guide to locate potential victims. Their targets consisted of high-level executives at some of America's largest companies. They would use *Who's Who* to develop the full name, birthdate and employment history of their target.

Additional research would then net them the home address, Social Security numbers, telephone numbers, and other data.

They would then begin the takeover of these people's identities. They netted millions of dollars before they were caught. Unlike most victims of identity theft, their targets possessed the resources and connections to motivate law enforcement authorities to actively investigate the case.

Television and movie stars are also vulnerable to identity theft. Although it is impractical for identity thieves to attempt to steal the identities of the biggest stars who have name and face recognition by most members of the public, the same is not true of the thousands of other television and movie stars who work regularly and make good money. These lesser known public figures are ripe targets. Anyone who performs regularly will earn a good income, which is one of the qualities the identity thief looks for.

The identity thief has two easy sources of information about these performers. The first is the series of industry directories that are published giving basic biographic and career data about most active members in the profession.

The second source is the performer's own publicity operation. Almost all performers have an address where fans can write them for autographed photographs and other information. This is especially true of lesser known performers, because this type of publicity can help develop a career.

The address given for such purposes is usually that of the actor's agent or manager. Quite often, this is also the address the performer uses for credit card applications, personal mail, and whenever a legal address is necessary for anything other than voting.

Where can the identity thief locate this address? There are numerous books published that tabulate the addresses of celebrities. These are available at most bookstores. Once the identity thief has this address, he can run a credit bureau header search to determine the Social Security number. Once he has this, the performer's identity is ripe for takeover by the criminal.

Anyone who has a high profile profession is particularly vulnerable to identity theft. This includes politicians, physicians, and business owners. One city council member in Los Angeles had her identity and that of her husband stolen. The thieves then used their names to purchase hundreds of thousands of dollars in luxury automobiles.

Almost any piece of personal data can be useful to identity thieves. One identity theft ring made a practice of stealing the identities of well off financial professionals on Wall Street in New York City. Where did they get the initial data to develop their target lists? From business cards.

They would call the firms where these individuals worked and pose as potential customers. The company would then mail more information, including a representative's business card. This was enough to begin the game.

Chapter Seven
The Different Types of Identity Thieves

Not all identity thieves have the same goals or objectives. Some identity theft is done by individuals acting alone, some is done by large, well financed organized criminal groups. Some groups that previously engaged in violent crimes now concentrate on identity theft because it is much less dangerous and financially very lucrative.

Many identity thieves have financial gain as their primary goal. They steal an individual's identity with the objective of looting all bank and credit accounts and then moving on. This is the most common type of identity thief.

Some identity thieves are looking for a chance to start over. This is typically an individual who has accumulated negative employment and credit records, perhaps is wanted for unpaid child support. This individual sees the theft of an identity as a way to put it all behind him, instantly.

This type of identity thief can be more dangerous than the first type because he might live for years under the victim's name. Eventually negative records may be created which would then start to affect the victim's life as well.

Then there is the evil minded identity thief. This identity thief steals the victim's identity with deliberate intent and malice. His goal is to cause the victim as much harm as possible, while racking up ill-gotten goods and cash.

This type of identity thief will quickly create arrest records and other negative records in the victim's name, perhaps in a town in another state. The victim first learns about the identity theft when the police come to arrest him.

In the next few chapters we will step inside the world of these different types of identity thieves, and follow them through their crimes, from beginning to end, and also see the fallout on the victims. Later, we will examine specific steps you can take to avoid becoming the victim of these crooks.

Chapter Eight
Identity Theft by Organized Crime

A doctor in Nebraska, a student in New York City, a New York subway toll collector, and a United Nations official all share one common experience. All of them were victims of identity theft of a well-organized, East Coast ring of identity thieves. They are not the only victims. Before the ring was shut down, more than one hundred people had their identities stolen.

Many of these victims still face ongoing problems related to the theft of their identity. The college student cannot convince a bank to open a checking account in her name, and some of the other victims find that they cannot obtain loans or mortgages. In some cases, even though the original identity theft ring has been closed down, the victims' personal identifiers have been sold off to other identity theft rings, and the victims are victimized a second time.

The crime begins with locating a group of potential victims. In this case, all of the victims shared the common trait: They either lived in or had visited New York City.

The doctor in Nebraska had attended a medical conference in New York. It is likely one of the identity theft gang members had obtained her business card. Identity thieves are known to target conferences where professionals gather. For an organized identity theft ring, paying a few hundred dollars admission to obtain access to a conference filled with hundreds or thousands of high-income professionals is a smart investment.

The United Nations official was targeted because of an article in *The New York Times*. This lesser official was quoted by name in the article, and that became the nucleus around which the ring located more information.

The student was targeted for a completely different reason. Most students have not enmeshed themselves in the credit system yet. As a result, banks are willing to approve credit cards for students who have no credit history under relaxed lending criteria. The student was located by an identity theft ring member searching through the student directory at a local university.

We could go on, but the tactics of the identity theft ring should be obvious. They locate information on desirable groups of individuals by any means possible. Another telltale sign of the organized identity theft ring is that they typically compile a master list of more than fifty people with skeleton identifiers.

The next step is to flesh out these profiles with additional information. The organized identity thieves will use local telephone directories or the Internet to locate the home address and telephone number of each person on their list. Anyone for whom they cannot locate a home address and telephone number is usually dropped at this point.

The next step is to then run these individuals, en masse, through an address lookup or national identifier program via an information broker. Once this search has been completed, the identity theft ring will have the birthdates, Social Security numbers, and employers of nearly everyone on the list. Anyone with little or no information is dropped from the list of potential victims.

The next step is to set up a network of addresses to receive mail in the names of the targets. Mail-forwarding services are generally not used because credit bureau warning programs will identify these addresses. Some rings will rent inexpensive apartments specifically for the purpose of receiving this mail. They will of course, use high quality fake ID to accomplish the rental. Sometimes they will rent the apartment in the name of the intended victim, using a piece of fake ID obtained in the victim's name.

If the apartment complex is one that does a credit check before renting, it only serves to help the identity theft ring. The credit check run by the apartment leasing company will cause the address on the credit report to be changed to the new, fraudulent address set up by the identity thieves.

Additional addresses will be created at secretarial services, which are not normally listed in credit bureau files. The next stage of preparation will be to obtain listed telephone numbers in the victims' names.

Credit grantors will sometimes still check to see if the credit applicant has a listed telephone number. It is very easy for the identity theft ring to obtain a telephone number listed in any name they choose.

Instead of contacting the telephone company, which would involve a credit check and detailed personal data, they use another source. Voice mail companies exist all over the United States and Canada, and many of them offer numbers nationwide in a number of different cities.

The voice mail company leases thousands of numbers at a time from local telephone companies. A switching center set up in each city where they operate acts as the "address" of the numbers. The voice mail company then resells these numbers to its customers.

If a customer wants the number listed with directory assistance, he pays an additional fee each month for this service. For around $50, the identity thief can get a listed telephone number anywhere in the country. The other beauty of a voice mail telephone number is that it leaves no traces. An investigator will again find no useful information by tracking calls made from the number, because no calls are ever made from the number, only to it.

Organized identity thieves even go one step further to protect their telephone numbers. All telephone calls made to the voice mail number to check for messages will be made from payphones located on busy thoroughfares far away from the actual location of the gang.

Now the preparation is complete. The final step, to use the stolen identities for financial gain, can now begin. The goal is to accumulate as much credit, merchandise and cash in the victims' names as quickly as possible. Once this is done, the identity will be collapsed by withdrawing all of the cash and maxing out the credit lines. Merchandise purchased with bad checks will be sold to pawn shops.

The organized identity theft gang will have a list of credit grantors. They will target bank credit cards first. They will have a list of creditors who offer applications via telephone, and are more lax about credit standards than others.

Applying for credit cards via telephone eliminates the need for a handwritten application, which means one less piece of evidence later on that can be used against the gang if they are caught. Telephone applications will also require less personal information than a long, printed application form. Of course, the telephone calls for all credit applications will be made from a payphone.

Other members of the gang, armed with fake ID, will hit up stores that sell easily fenced, big ticket items, such as computer and video equipment. They will apply for instant credit at these stores. Credit is notoriously easy to get at such places, with very high credit lines.

The high interest rates on these merchant cards, often in excess of 20 percent, and the desire to sell expensive items, will get an applicant with good credit a credit line in excess of $5,000 in just a few minutes.

The identity thieves will then go purchase merchandise right up to the value of the credit line. In many cases, the gang will have a buyer already lined up to purchase the new computer or big screen television.

The organized ring will also know which credit bureau a particular creditor uses. This way, they can spread out the credit applications between creditors that use different bureaus. This is important, because once four or more inquiries have been made against a credit report in a six month period, most credit grantors will not approve any new applications. They will send a rejection letter saying that they cannot approve any new credit because of excessive inquiries on the credit report.

By spreading out the applications between the three bureaus, the gang can hit victims up to nine times before rejections start coming in.

The next phase of the operation involves opening up checking accounts at various banks. This will be very easy to do. Armed with a fake ID and a few hundred dollars, gang members will go to different branches of banks actively soliciting new accounts.

Most banks will call one of the check verification services to make sure the applicant does not have a reputation of writing bad paper all over town. Once this check comes back clean, the account will be be opened. Most banks call or computer link with the check-clearing firm while the applicant is waiting. It only takes a few seconds.

The identity thief now walks out of the bank with a fistful of starter checks, and in a week will receive an ATM card and checks printed with the victim's name in the mail.

The checking account serves two purposes. Later, toward the end of the game, the account will be used to purchase big ticket items with checks that later bounce. In the short term, it aids the credit card scheme.

Most credit cards come with convenience checks, which can be used for a cash advance. Instead of having to wait a few weeks for a code to use the ATM with the credit card, the identity thief can immediately start to deplete the credit line for cash by writing one of these checks and depositing it into his bank account, the fraudulent one set up for this purpose.

With particularly credit worthy victims, the identity thieves can even arrange a second mortgage on the victim's house or obtain signature lines of credit.

There will come a time to burn out the victim's credit. Over a period of a few weeks, all of the credit lines will be maxed out. At the very end, checks will be written to purchase such items as jewelry and home electronics.

Before the checks bounce, the gang will abandon the apartment they rented for this purpose. Some identity thieves never even physically enter the apartment. They simply collect their mail. This leaves no evidence, such as discarded papers or fingerprints, if the case ever gets seriously investigated. The mailbox is wiped clean on the last visit.

The victim will find out a few days later when he starts to get angry calls at work from merchants where "his" checks have bounced. This is the beginning of months of hell for the victim, and the end of the game, at least for this name, for the organized identity theft ring.

Chapter Nine
The Long-Term Identity Thief

Bradley Peterson had a problem. He wanted to live a lifestyle beyond his means. Lots of things were difficult for Brad. He had trouble renting decent apartments because of his poor credit history. He always had to live in rat traps where the owners did not check out a tenant's background.

He was a smart guy, but the discipline to complete a college degree or trade school just was not in him. He was jealous of his high school classmates who had gone on to college and now had good jobs.

He could not get credit cards, and his love life was in the toilet. He could barely afford to date girls on what he earned at his minimum-wage job at the Chicken Shack. Life was not looking too good for this 27-year-old man.

But Bradley had one thing going for him: His innate intelligence. Even without a formal education, he could probably do well in a sales job that required a degree, or any job where you learned after you were hired. He just could never get his foot in the door.

Brad went to his tenth high school reunion, and saw buddies from a decade ago. Most of the guys he had hung out with had gotten serious, finished college or graduate school, and now had successful jobs. He collected business cards and addresses from his old cronies, and the nucleus of a plan began to form in his mind.

Why not become one of his more successful friends? He could then get the good job, live in a nice apartment, and go out with good-looking women. It was so easy to do.

A call to his school's alumni office netted him the birthdates and current addresses of his old chums. He then called them up on the telephone, pretending to be chatting casually about the old days, but in reality asking some detailed questions.

He found out where and when they attended college, and what their majors were. He learned where they were born, and where their parents were from. He had seen how this was done in a movie and, surprisingly, it actually worked.

Brad relocated to sunny California, got the good job, swanky apartment and pretty girl. He lived the good life for about a year until it all came crashing down. Returning from a trip to Europe, he was asked at U.S. Immigration to step aside for a few minutes. Those few minutes wound up consuming the next eighteen months of his life in a federal minimum-security prison.

Bradley Peterson is an example of a different type of identity thief. Unlike the organized crime identity thieves who have a quick financial killing as their motivation, the long-term identity thief has different motives.

You might be wondering how Bradley Peterson was caught. He made a critical mistake when he obtained a passport in his victim's name. Passports are issued by only one agency, the U.S. State Department.

When someone applies for a new passport, the state department checks its records to see if this person has already been issued a passport. This is how Brad was caught. His victim applied for a passport after Brad had already obtained one. The passport office investigated and realized the passport issued to Brad was fraudulent.

Brad's passport was immediately invalidated, and the passport number was entered into the "lookout" file maintained by the U.S. Immigration and Naturalization Service at all ports of entry. When Brad attempted to pass through customs, the jig was up.

The long-term identity thief wants to jettison his past and all of its negative records, and start all over, again. He can do this by one of two methods. One is to create a brand new identity from scratch. This is one option many choose, but it takes a long time to execute, and careful planning.

The simpler method is to steal the identity of an individual who is living the type of life the identity thief would like to have. Frequently, in these cases, the victims are friends, relatives, acquaintances, or business colleagues of the identity thief.

The long-term identity thief will attempt to obtain duplicate educational transcripts and the birth certificate of the victim. As we saw in the case of Brad, this is very simple to do when the potential victims are not total strangers to the thief.

Conversations with the victims are carefully steered in the direction to produce information such as birthdates and other personal data. A co-worker's wallet or purse might be rifled through to learn other information such as drivers license numbers and Social Security numbers.

Questions about foreign travel can be manipulated to learn if the victim has ever obtained a passport. Only a few foreign countries, such as Canada, Mexico, and some Caribbean nations can be visited without a passport.

Other information will be developed, such as all the different states where the victim has lived, and where there might be other relatives. Once this data has been accumulated, the long-term identity thief is ready to strike.

Most of the time the long-term identity thief will pick a state far away from where the victim lives. This reduces the possibility of clerks asking nasty questions in state agencies when a search turns up an existing or past drivers license or other documents in the victim's name.

The long-term identity thief will rent an apartment in the name of the victim. Because the victim has good credit and other references, the rental will proceed smoothly. After this is done, the long-term identity thief will go about obtaining "soft" identity documents in the victim's name.

The thief will apply for a voter registration card, along with a library card. The identity thief will join one of the warehouse shopping clubs that issues photo identification. He may even register for a class at a local university or community college to obtain a photographic student identity card.

Once armed with these documents, he will proceed to the motor vehicle department and apply for a state identification card. He will show the duplicate birth certificate, along with some supporting identification, which he now has in abundance.

The Motor Vehicle Department will not show any current license or identity card issued in this name, and a check of the National Driver Register of drivers with suspended or revoked licenses will yield nothing. In a few weeks, he can come back and obtain a drivers license itself.

The next step is to open a bank account. He will go to a local bank and present the state identification card and one other piece of supportive documentation. The bank will call a check verification service and be told that no negative data exists in its files for this person. The account will be opened, and a few days later an ATM card and printed checks will arrive at the identity thief's address.

Obtaining credit is the next step. The identity thief will have little or no trouble obtaining a major credit card in the name of his victim. This is especially true if the card issuer uses the same credit bureau that was consulted by the apartment rental company. The inquiry by the apartment rental firm will have already altered the address on the credit report.

Arranging for telephone service will be very easy. The identity thief simply calls the local telephone company and provides them with the victim's name, Social Security number, and past telephone number.

The telephone company representative then calls the previous local telephone company and asks about his bill payment history. Assuming the payment history is good, the identity thief will be able to obtain telephone service without a deposit of any kind.

In some areas, telephone companies will install local telephone service without requiring any type of references; only a connection fee is required. The limitations with these services are that direct dial long distance calls can't be made, and no one can call in collect.

It's easy to arrange employment. The identity thief is armed with the educational credentials and transcripts of his victim. The only problem the identity thief faces is that he cannot give the actual current employer of his victim as a reference. He can, however, list former employers of his victim as references.

The enterprising identity thief will get around this little problem easily. He will simply arrange a dummy employment reference in a far off city. He will rent a mail-forwarding service address in that city, along with an answering service telephone number. He will have letterheads printed up in the name of this dummy firm.

Attached to his resume will be a detailed letter of reference from this dummy corporation. The recipient of the résumé will be invited to call if any additional information is needed. This will be the answering service number, which will be answered in the name of the dummy corporation. The caller will be told that the letter writer is out, but to leave his number and his call will be returned soon. Of course, the individual returning the call will be the identity thief, vouching for his own reference.

The long-term identity thief can live for many years as a duplicate of a real individual, if he avoids certain mistakes. It is absolutely necessary that the identity thief relocate himself far away from his namesake. Detection will surely follow if the true individual moves to the state where the identity thief is living.

Careful detective work must be done by the identity thief. If it is the identity thief's goal to live in Washington State, he must investigate his target carefully to determine that his intended victim would never have any obvious interest in moving to the Evergreen State.

He needs to find out where the intended victim's wife is from, where her parents live, and where the intended victim likes to vacation. Then avoid these locales. A favorite vacation spot can later become a place to relocate.

The other problem involves the Internal Revenue Service and taxes. The long-term identity thief cannot work under the Social Security number of his victim. This will lead to rapid detection. If both the victim and the identity thief are working under the same Social Security number, there will be a problem at tax time.

The victim will report the income he earns, but not the additional money his namesake is earning across the country.

After the real individual files his tax returns, he will receive a nasty letter asking why he failed to declare this additional income earned in another state. This will start the beginning of the end of the identity thief's new life.

There are two potential ways around this problem for the identity thief. The first is to incorporate a business, and sell his services that way. This is a very popular option for an identity thief who wants to work as a commissioned salesperson, or who wishes to sell professional services, such as computer skills, to an employer.

The corporation is assigned an employer identification number by the Internal Revenue Service. The checks are made payable to the corporation, and the corporation files an income tax return each year. As the owner of the corporation, the identity thief simply withdraws funds from the company to meet his expenses.

The second method, which is more applicable to identity thieves who work for a traditional paycheck, was created by the Internal Revenue Service. This method allows the identity thief to obtain what is known as a ITIN, or Individual Taxpayer Identification Number directly from the Internal Revenue Service.

This number is not a Social Security number; rather, it's a number that was created to recognize that there are more than four million illegal immigrants living in the United States, and most of them hold jobs.

This number allows illegal immigrants and anyone else who does not want to get a Social Security number to earn a salary and claim income tax deductions. If a refund is due, it will be paid. This is not the case if someone works under a made up Social Security number.

A tax return bearing an incorrect Social Security number will have all deductions on it disallowed by the Internal Revenue Service. The identification number was introduced as a way to encourage illegal aliens to get into the income tax system and pay their fair share.

Appendix Four contains a reproduction of the application form for this number and the instructions that accompany it.

The long-term identity thief would simply apply for this number using the new state identification card or drivers license obtained in the victim's name.

The long-term identity thief can cause many more potential problems for the victim than the organized crime identity thieves. The organized identity thieves have one goal — quick financial gain. Once they have milked the victim's identity for all they can extract from it, they move on to their next victim.

The long-term identity thief is building a second life under the victim's identity. As time goes by, this second life becomes more and more real, with more and more files being created such as banking records, payroll records, voter registration, motor vehicle, and tenancy records.

What happens if the long-term identity thief gets married in the victim's name, or fathers an out-of-wedlock child, and the mother demands child support? This has happened on more than a few occasions.

Consider the long-term identity thief who gets a woman pregnant, but refuses to support the child. The identity thief moves on to a different state to avoid being harassed by the mother of the baby.

The mother contacts the state child support agency, and they initiate paternity proceedings against the identity thief. Eventually, a judgment for unpaid child support and, possibly an arrest warrant are issued.

One day, the victim, on the other side of the country, is pulled over by the police for a routine speeding ticket. The police officer runs his name through the wanted persons database, and — bingo — up pops the arrest warrant for unpaid child support.

The victim is going to jail. The burden will be on him to prove that the out-of-state warrant is erroneous and the result of fraud. Only if the victim can afford a lawyer will he be able to avoid being extradited to the state that issued the warrant.

The same problem can creep up if the impostor accumulates civil judgments in the victim's name. The real individual may find his wages garnisheed because of a judgment a creditor has gotten on the other side of the country.

Even worse problems can befall the victim if the impostor creates a criminal record in another state. The real person could lose a professional license, have trouble entering foreign countries, or be subject to arrest because he is violating some condition of parole or probation to which his Doppelgänger is subject.

The real person could face loss of insurance. If the impostor was convicted of drunk driving in another state, eventually the victim's insurance company may find out about it, and cancel his policy. If the impostor is kicked out of an apartment because of failure to pay rent, the real individual may find it impossible to obtain living space.

As dangerous as the long-term identity thief is to his victim, there is even a more sinister type of identity thief. This type of identity thief purposely decides to wreck the identity of the victim. This thief will create, by design, as many negative records as possible in the name of the victim. In the next chapter we will see how this thief operates.

Chapter Ten
The Malevolent Identity Thief

Nan Farnell was a clerk at the Washington State Department of Licensing. Each day she would help numerous people apply for new drivers licenses, or renew existing ones. Nan, in her early 40s, found the job to be somewhat boring — it was the same thing day after day. The pay was good, but not what she thought she should be earning at this phase in her life.

Many of the clients she helped earned more money than she did, and had nicer cars to prove it. Nan decided that it was time to even up the score, and take some of these stuck-up people down a notch. Nan hatched an ingenious plan; one that would cause some of her victims serious problems with the law in the near future.

As a motor vehicle clerk, Nan was privy to all of the personal information about her clients. She knew their full names, birthdates, mother's maiden name, drivers license number, and a host of other information. Nan realized she could steal the identities of these women at will, and then commit all sorts of crimes with little or no chance of being caught.

The first step was to single out those clients who bore a general resemblance to her. The women did not need to be a spitting image of her, but just have similar height, weight, eye and hair color, and age.

Whenever a woman would come to her station with these characteristics, she would make a note of the person, and run a duplicate copy of their licensing file. She also purchased a home laminator, and stole blank license stock from her employer. With these supplies, she was in business.

At home she would print up a second license in the name of her chosen victim. She would then affix her photograph to the license document in place of the real woman's. Her fake licenses looked just like the real ones because the stock they were printed on was genuine and she used the same system to process them that was used at her job.

The license number and expiration and issue dates were all authentic; a police computer check would show it to be valid. Now the crime spree could begin. Nan was out to milk these identities for everything she could get out of them.

Immediately, Nan opened up checking accounts all over town. She fancied expensive jewelry and wrote numerous checks at high-end jewelers all over the Seattle area. Each check would be approved because the women she had targeted had good credit histories and check writing patterns.

Then the checks started to bounce, and one jeweler who had been ripped off for a particularly large amount decided to obtain his money or get satisfaction under the law.

The jeweler called the real woman listed on the check, asking her to make good. The victim told the jeweler that she must be mistaken, that she had never visited her store or made a purchase there. The angry jeweler then called the police and filed a felony theft complaint.

The next day the police arrested the victim, even though she steadfastly denied writing the check. The coup de grace happened when the jeweler positively identified the woman as being the check fraud artist. Felony charges were filed and the woman was subsequently convicted of the offense.

While awaiting sentencing in jail, the victim caught a lucky break. Nan Farnell was still up to her tricks. A different woman had been victimized, and told almost an identical story to the police. This new victim also had no criminal record and was an upstanding citizen. It was only then that the police realized that an identity thief was at work, and that the woman who was about to be sent to a state prison was in fact innocent, and also the victim of a crime.

The reader may wonder about the visual identification the jewelry store owner made of the victim. Identity thieves count on the folly of human recognition. Writing a check is a very brief transaction. If all goes according to routine procedures, the person accepting the check will have no need to remember the check writer's appearance in any real detail. What is remembered from short encounters like this one are the general outlines of someone's looks, such as the height, weight, hair color, and eye color. These are precisely the identifiers that Nan Farnell made sure she matched before embarking on her scheme.

Nan Farnell is an example of the most dangerous type of identity thief — the kind who deliberately sets out to cause harm and ruin to her victims. These identity thieves are known to obtain criminal records and warrants in the name of their victims. They do so without worry, because once the stolen identity becomes too hot to use anymore, they simply move on to another, or resume using their real names.

The danger for the victim, lacking any documentation to the contrary, is that the criminal record can come back to haunt him at times when he is least expecting it.

Job applications might fall through. An employer might perform a background check, discover this conviction, and fire the employee on the spot for not being honest about his past.

The police may arrest him, and hold him until he has been extradited back to another state to stand trial for a felony warrant outstanding in his name. Child support workers might have part of his paycheck garnisheed to help support illegitimate children fathered in another state.

The victim must act quickly in the case of the malevolent identity thief, because his very freedom might be in peril. The second the victim gets any inkling that his identity has been compromised, he needs to report it to the local police agency at once. A copy of this police report should be carried on the victim at all times.

All drivers licenses, bank accounts, telephone numbers, and other accounts and identification information need to be changed. This will prevent current accounts of the victim from being taken over. The credit bureaus need to be notified, and other steps taken that we will discuss in more detail in the following chapters.

How does the malevolent identity thief obtain personal data about her victims? Nan Farnell's case was unique because of her high level of access to sensitive information. Most malevolent identity thieves obtain data by different means.

Some of these identity thieves obtain personal data from job or credit applications. One malevolent identity thief who worked for a major department store chain secretly photocopied the credit applications of all new customers in the store. These applications became the grist for later rip-offs. One disgruntled store clerk used the employment application of her boss to run up unpaid bills all over town. The store subsequently fired the victim.

The best way to stop all three types of identity thieves is to avoid becoming a victim of one of them in the first place. In the next chapter we will examine some specific strategies to lessen the risk that your identity will be stolen.

Chapter Eleven
Avoiding Identity Thieves

There are certain steps individuals can take to avoid becoming the victims of identity thieves. These steps involve making an ongoing commitment to protect personal data privacy. This will involve making certain changes in the way the person lives and handles personal information.

Unfortunately, there are no absolutes. If a professional group of identity thieves has targeted you, there is very little you can do to stop them from victimizing you. The best protection is to control your personal information so well that you slip below the radar screen to where only family and close friends can locate you.

We have seen how an identity thief can learn your Social Security number with only a name and address. This is the common method used by professional, organized rings of identity thieves to locate potential high-income victims.

The first step in securing your identity is to remove your actual home address and telephone number from circulation.

You will need to obtain an alternative mailing address. You have two choices: A post office box, or a private mailbox service, such as Mail Boxes Etc. For most people, the second choice is better.

A private mailbox service allows you to use their street address as your own. The box number becomes a suite number. For many documents, agencies will want a street address, not a post office box. A mailbox service address provides this.

Another alternative to the private mailbox service is the secretarial or office space rental service. These services will cost a little bit more than a private mailbox service, but you will get the same benefit of an actual street address to receive your mail.

Once you have rented an alternative mailing address, this becomes your legal address for all third party paperwork. Items such as job applications, motor vehicle paperwork, bank account statements, and magazine subscriptions, will all be sent to this address.

You can also enhance your privacy when dealing with third parties by using a spurious name when getting magazine or catalog subscriptions to this address. Mail-service operators will allow you to use any name you wish on your box, or more than one name, so long as all mail has the correct box number on it.

By using a spurious name for magazine and catalog subscriptions, you keep your name out of the databases compiled by marketing companies. The same is true if you fill out a warranty card for an expensive purchase.

Warranty cards are processed by marketing companies which use the information given on them to compile a list of users of the company's products, and individual profiles of each user. By sending in a warranty card with a mail-service address, and a spurious name, you stay out of these databases.

To get your address and telephone number removed from direct mailing marketing lists, you will need to send a letter to the association listed below. Once you have sent a letter to this group, all member companies will remove your name and address from their files within a few months. The address is:

Mail Preference Service
Direct Marketing Association
PO Box 9008
Farmingdale, NY 11735

The next part of our plan involves removing your personal data from the single largest source of personal information available: the telephone directory. Having your telephone number and address listed in the local phone book does not only get you listed in your local community. Numerous CD-ROM databases of telephone numbers and addresses are compiled from local telephone books nationwide. Many of these databases will also provide the user with a map of directions to your address. To say out of these databases, call the telephone company and get your number changed, and also have this number made non-published. A non-published number will not only not come up when requested from directory assistance or be listed in the telephone book, it will also not show up in something known as a reverse directory.

One type of database firms use is a reverse directory. A reverse directory lists telephone numbers by address, not by number. A simple unlisted number will show up in a reverse directory. A non-published number will not.

Once you have this new number, it should only be given to family members and close friends. This number will not be used for any other purpose. You will need to obtain a second number for all other purposes.

This second number will not be obtained from the telephone company. New technology has created a new generation of telecommunications suppliers known as voice mail companies. These companies rent numbers in bulk from the local telephone company and then resell them to members of the public. They can also set up numbers that allow callers to leave messages of several minutes in length, and that will ring the client's pager when a call comes through. This is the option I recommend.

The voice mail number will be rented in the name and address of your mail service. You should obtain a pager so that you can return calls at once. This can be set up quickly and will cost around $20 per month.

When making calls from your actual home telephone, be aware of Caller ID. If you call someone who has this service, they can learn your non-published telephone number easily. Make sure you obtain Caller ID blocking when you obtain your new telephone number. Beware however, that this does not always work when you call toll-free numbers. Marketing companies and companies that sell via toll-free numbers usually have software to capture your telephone number when you call to place an order or ask for information. Make all calls to places such as these from your work telephone or a pay phone.

The next step of our identity theft avoidance plan involves changing how you do your banking. The use of personal checks as a form of payment at stores must stop. Every time you write a personal check you are issuing an open invitation to identity thieves.

One organized identity theft ring offered store clerks a $20 payment for reporting the personal information recorded on a check. A personal check provides an identity thief with most of the information he needs to begin, plus the valuable bank account number and signature.

Some banks make it very easy for identity thieves to determine how much money you keep in your account. One of the ten largest banks in the United States allows anyone to call an automated account information line. The caller simply selects the account rating option and enters in the account number from the check. The bank will tell the caller the amount of money in the account in an ever increasing range of tens.

The computer tells the caller if he has less than $1,000, between $1,000 and $10,000, or more than $10,000 in an account.

The caller is not screened. There is no need for an identification number; anyone with your checking account number can call.

In addition to no longer writing checks at merchants, it is probably an excellent idea to close out your current checking account and open a new one at a different bank.

Check-verification services, such as Telecheck and Scan, do more than simply approve your check. They also collect and sell personal data about you. If you have ever written a check at a merchant who uses one of these services, your bank account data is already being bandied about in cyberspace, ripe for the picking by identity thieves.

One must understand exactly how check-authorization services work to see why they traffic in customer information. Contrary to popular belief, check-verification services do not actually call your bank to verify that you have the money in your account. Check-verification services essentially sell merchants insurance against having to collect on bad checks.

Check-verification services know that the vast majority of checks are good, and most checks that bounce are made good the second time they are presented to banks. A small merchant, however, can be affected harshly by even a few bounced checks, especially if one of the checks is for a large amount. Bounced checks also create the expense of having to hire someone to call the check writers and cajole them into making their bad paper good.

The check-verification service eliminates all of these problems. In return for only accepting checks that meet the criteria of the clearing service and paying a percentage of all accepted checks to the clearing agency, the clearing service agrees to make good on any checks that bounce to the merchant. The check-verification service is actually selling insurance.

To reduce the risk of accepting bad checks, the check-verification service attempts to build up a database of information on all check writers. Those who write bad checks and do not make them good will soon find that no merchant will accept their checks, and that they cannot open up new bank checking accounts.

Every time a customer writes a check at a merchant that uses a check clearing service, the bank account number, check number, identification type and number, and the amount of the check are submitted to the database via an authorization terminal. This information is then checked for a match against the file of people who have had their check writing privileges suspended. If a match occurs, the check is denied. If no match occurs, the check is approved and the merchant is given an authorization code to write on the check.

Alternatives to checks are cash, debit, and ATM cards, credit cards, and traveler's checks. Traveler's checks are an especially good form of check substitutes because they can be reimbursed if lost or stolen. If you buy traveler's checks in ten- and twenty-dollar denominations, you will find that you have no difficulty using them at most places where you formerly used checks.

Traveler's checks can be purchased fee free after joining the American Automobile Association, as a membership benefit.

Debit and ATM cards also allow you to eliminate writing checks at places where you would not want to use a traveler's check. Essentially, your use of checks should be confined to paying bills by mail. Do not have drivers license and telephone numbers preprinted on your checks. In fact, if the only use you make of your checks is paying household bills by mail, you can use starter checks, or checks that contain no personal information on them to conduct your business.

The biggest destroyer of personal privacy, and single most valuable piece of information for an identity thief is your Social Security number. With this number numerous records about you can be accessed very easily. This is due to the use of the Social Security number as a file identification tool by many different government agencies and private businesses.

Why has everyone decided to use the Social Security number as a file identifier? It is because of the very nature of the number itself. Each Social Security number was originally intended to identify a particular retirement account held by the federal government in trust for the individual.

A numbering system needed to be created that could identify each American worker uniquely, even if hundreds of people happened to have the same name and birthdate. The Social Security number thus became a man-made fixed identifier — one that does not change over the life of the individual. Appendix Two includes more information about the structure of the Social Security number.

Clearly then, one can reduce the chances of becoming a victim of identity theft by reducing how many other agencies and businesses have access to the Social Security number.

The first steps are simple in this regard. Do not carry your Social Security card in your wallet or purse. If this card is lost, or an identity thief sees it, your privacy is blown wide open. Keep your Social Security card at home with other important papers in a secure location.

If your Social Security number appears on your drivers license, or is used as the license number, have it removed or changed. Many states are now allowing people to do this because of the increasing amount of identity theft. Also have the address changed on the license to that of your mail service address.

Be wary of using your Social Security number or part of it as a code to access your personal accounts. Many banks, universities, and stock brokerage firms use the last four digits of your Social Security number as a password. Demand that an alternative password be used of your own making, and avoid numerical combinations that involve your birthdate or the birthdates of your spouse or children.

Many utility companies want your Social Security number before initiating service, as do some cable television providers. Some of these firms do this because they run a credit check. See if alternative arrangements can be made if you agree to pay a deposit in lieu of a credit check.

Whenever a private business asks for your Social Security number, remember that they have no legal right to the number. You might have to be firm about this and ask to speak with a supervisor.

Make sure that you shred all unnecessary correspondence that contains your Social Security number. One low-tech way identity thieves obtain Social Security numbers is by searching through the garbage of upscale apartments or businesses. By using greater care with your garbage, you can eliminate this avenue of fraud.

Never use your mother's maiden name as a password. Identity thieves can and will obtain your birth certificate, and then have this identifier. Instead of your mother's maiden name, use that of a favorite pet or cartoon character. The mother's maiden name is such a strong identifier that when an identity thief knows this information about you, all doubt in the mind of the financial services provider he is attempting to defraud is removed. The mother's maiden name has allowed many identity thieves to loot the pension funds of their victims or make withdrawals from tax-deferred annuity accounts.

Make sure that the address on your car registration is changed to that of your mail service. One way identity thieves target upscale victims is to write down the license plate numbers of cars they see in parking lots. Later, they order a copy of the vehicle registration certificate via an information broker. This will give them the registered owner's name and address, which, as we have seen, is all that is necessary to steal a stranger's identity.

Make it clear that you expect your personal information to be protected with all businesses you deal with. Tell them you do not want your personal information sold or rented out to other companies. Get this promise in writing, and make it clear that you will take your business elsewhere if the business does not comply with your wishes. Appendix Four includes a sample letter demanding that a private business do just this.

Restricting who can see your credit report is the single largest enhancement you can make to your credit privacy. All three of the major credit bureaus allow credit grantors access to information in your file without you being a customer of theirs, or requesting credit from them.

This practice is called prescreening. Prescreening allows the credit bureaus to dance around any restrictions imposed upon them by the Fair Credit Reporting Act.

Prescreening involves the credit bureau mining their files for common traits that a credit grantor may find to be desirable. A credit card company might tell a credit bureau that it wants a list of 100,000 people in the state of Colorado who earn more than $50,000 per year, own a home, and have at least two existing premium credit cards with limits of at least $10,000.

The credit bureau will then search its database to identify these consumers. What will be generated is a list of names and addresses that meet this criteria. The credit card company can specify any criteria it wants, so long as it is information the bureau has in its files.

Because the credit report itself is not seen, the credit card company does not have to get the consent of the consumers whose credit histories were electronically grazed to compile the list. This list is then used to send out pre-approved credit card offers to the individuals named thereon.

Prescreening lists themselves create opportunity for identity thieves. Any company can purchase these lists directly from a credit bureau or from a third party vendor. These lists can also be resold to another company once they have been used by the first buyer. Each additional trip the list makes increases the chance that people named on it will become victims of identity theft.

Fortunately, you can prevent your credit report from being used for prescreening purposes. In reaction to much negative publicity and changes in both federal and state credit reporting laws, the three major bureaus have made it easy to opt out of prescreening.

You can call each of the three major bureaus at the numbers given below and tell them that you want to opt out of prescreening. The representative on the telephone will take the necessary steps to see that this happens. In addition to the telephone call, you will want to send a letter to the credit bureau as well requesting that this be done. Cite the date of your telephone call and the name of the individual you dealt with in the letter. A sample opt out letter appears in Appendix Four.

One phone call to (800) 353-0809 works for all the major bureaus' opt-out programs. The addresses are:

Equifax
P.O. Box 740241
Atlanta, GA 30374

Experian
P.O. Box 949
Allen, TX 75013

Trans Union
P.O. Box 390
Springfield, PA 19064

The steps outlined in this chapter can go a long way toward reducing your chances of becoming the victim of identity thieves. It requires some commitment, but the reward is a much reduced chance of ever having to endure the hell that identity-theft victims suffer. In the next chapter we will see what steps must be taken if you have already become the victim of identity thieves.

Chapter Twelve
Fighting Back After Victimization

Despite taking all precautions, you could still become a victim of identity thieves. The amount of disruption you face in your life, and the duration of same, will depend in large part on how rapidly you respond to the first signs of the impending crisis.

Your first warning that you have become the victim of identity theft will probably be a telephone call from a bank or other creditor asking when you will be making payment on an overdue account. The bank will not be one that you can remember ever doing business with.

The proper response to a telephone call such as this is to obtain as much information as possible from the caller. You will want to know the following information:

- the bank or creditor name
- the account number
- account balance
- when the account was opened
- address where billing statements are sent
- ask for a copy of the original credit application

Inform the caller that you have been the victim of identity theft. Obtain his name and address. Follow up the call with a letter stating the same fact. A sample of the type of letter that should be written to creditors is given in Appendix Four.

The bank's fraud department will send you an affidavit to sign and return. This affidavit will simply state that you did not authorize the account and that it was fraudulently opened in your name. Some banks will want this notarized. Make a copy of the affidavit and send it to the bank via certified mail, return receipt requested.

You will need to get a file folder, and keep copies of each letter sent to a credit grantor. Individual folders for each bank or credit grantor is an even better idea. This allows you to track all correspondence. With each affidavit sent out, enclose a second letter requesting that the fraudulent account be removed from your credit report immediately.

After this first credit grantor contacts you, you should not wait for other calls to come in. Within a few weeks numerous creditors will be calling and demanding payment. You must be proactive, and get on top of the situation.

The next step is to call all three of the major credit bureaus on their fraud hotline telephone number listed in Chapter Eleven. Do not expect the credit bureaus to feel your situation is as dire or urgent as you do. They receive hundreds of telephone calls daily from victims; to them, your misfortune is simply a cost of doing business.

Before you call, make a list of all of your credit grantors, including balances for credit card accounts, mortgages, personal loans, and car payments. The fraud representative will go through your credit report line by line with you and identify all accounts. If there are accounts on your credit report you do not recall opening, the fraud representative will delete them.

You will also need to obtain the account numbers and phone numbers of the issuers of these fraudulent accounts. You should then contact these credit grantors directly and then send them a follow up letter stating that these accounts were opened up fraudulently in your name and to have them removed from your credit report.

Have each credit bureau fax you a copy of your credit report, clearly showing all of the fraudulent accounts. Once you have done this you will need to avoid the peril of being falsely arrested for crimes committed by someone else in your name.

Take copies of all of your correspondence to your local police department. Tell them that you have been the victim of identity theft and want to file a report. Unfortunately, the response from your local police will vary widely.

Some police departments are well-versed on identity theft, will make a report at once, and will provide you with excellent advice on what additional steps you need to take. Other departments will have to be pressured into making a report at all.

This is due to the legal situation regarding identity theft. In many states, the theft of your identity is not in and of itself a crime. Obtaining credit under false pretenses is; however, the creditor, not you, is considered the victim.

Press to get a report made for your own security. Once you have the police report, keep a copy on your person at all times. If a warrant is later issued in your name, for passing bad checks (or another crime) and you are pulled over, a copy of the police report may convince the officer that you are the victim and not the actual criminal. Indeed, it may be the only thing that keeps you out of jail.

The United States Secret Service is the federal agency having jurisdiction over identity theft cases. They do not get involved unless the identity theft has caused massive losses, as will be the case if your identity was stolen by a ring of organized criminals.

The problem is that the pattern of an identity theft ring in operation often does not show up until months later, after numerous individuals and banks have been hit. Only then, will the Secret Service assign officers to investigate.

Sometimes, if the victim contacts the Secret Service directly, they will also take a report. The same can be done with the U.S. Postal Service.

It is a violation of federal postal laws to use the mails to send false credit applications, or to obtain fraudulently issued credit cards via the U.S. Postal Service. Contact the local postal inspector. She can make a report and actually investigate the address where the cards were delivered. In fact, the Postal Service is often more willing to investigate identity theft cases than any other agency.

This is the other reality of identity theft cases. Very little real investigation of individual cases is done. Unless the losses to a particular credit grantor are very large, most agencies simply make a report and that is the effective end of the matter.

Most credit grantors consider losses due to identity theft as just another cost of business, akin to charged-off accounts. It would cost the credit grantors more to hire staff to actively investigate cases and develop evidence that could be used to obtain convictions of identity thieves.

Local police departments face the same cost-versus-benefit tradeoff. Identity theft is not a crime of violence, and the losses in each individual case are small — not hundreds of thousands or millions of dollars. Identity theft cases require lots of time and patience to put together evidence, and the lack of cooperation from the credit grantors makes it more difficult.

Once a case is put together, the district attorney may decline to prosecute, or plead the case out to a minor charge. Court dockets are overflowing, and resources must be devoted to crimes of violence.

It is up to you, the victim, to get your life back again. Filing the necessary reports with law enforcement is done not to catch the thieves, but to protect you from going to jail for their activities in your name.

Dealing with creditors and the credit bureaus is only the beginning. The identity thieves may have opened checking accounts in your name. You will need to contact the major check-clearing agencies and advise them that you have been the victim of identity theft and need to know if they have any adverse information in their files under your name and identification number.

If bad information surfaces, find out the bank's name and phone number, and the fraudulent account number. Contact the bank directly and advise them that this account was opened fraudulently in your name and that you are the victim of identity theft. Send the branch manager a copy of your police report. Ask that the bank stop reporting this account to the check-guarantee service and credit bureaus as overdrawn and closed by the bank.

You will want to send a similar "I am an identity theft victim" letter to each of the major check-clearing agencies along with a copy of the police report. The fraud numbers at the check-clearing services are:

- Telecheck: (800)-710-9898

- Scan: (800)-262-7771

- Chexsystems: (800)-428-9623

- Equifax: (888)-909-7304

- Checkrite: (800)-766-2748

- National Processing Company: (800)-526-5380

After you have taken these steps with the check-clearing companies and credit bureaus, you will want to begin the process of changing your personal identifiers so you cannot be revictimized again. Even though a fraud block is now on your credit report, your drivers license number and Social Security number are still in the hands of the identity thieves.

Go visit your motor vehicle department and tell them that you have been the victim of identity theft. Take a copy of your police report and other documentation with you. You will be required to fill out some paperwork, and a new license will be issued. Make sure that the number on the new license is *different* than the old license number. This will allow you to reenter the banking system.

The next stop is the Social Security office. You must get a new Social Security number. Your efforts to free yourself of the millstone of the identity thieves will be useless unless you obtain a new Social Security number.

You will need to prove to the Social Security office that misuse of your current Social Security number played an integral role in the identity theft. Copies of your credit reports and police report will suffice. The Social Security people will have you fill out a new application, and you will receive your new card in about two weeks. They will link your earnings history under your old number to the new number so you will not lose any benefits.

You can now create a new credit history with this new number. This is better than having your current accounts transferred over. Many times this will result in the credit bureau transferring over the fraudulent accounts onto the new credit report. Obtain a secured credit card and slowly rebuild a new credit history untainted by the old information.

Having the old, fraudulent accounts creep back onto your credit report frequently happens in identity theft cases. The credit bureau removes the fraudulent accounts when you call in to report the fraud. A month later, the creditor sends the credit bureau a listing of all accounts. The fraudulent account is reinserted in the credit report because the creditor forgot to remove the account from their monthly reporting cycle.

If this happens to you, write a threatening letter to both the credit bureau and the creditor. Tell them if this is not immediately remedied, you will report them to the Federal Trade Commission and institute legal action.

The Federal Trade Commission is the organization that regulates credit bureaus and check-clearing agencies. If you do not get expeditious responses to your problems, write to the FTC, enclosing copies of the police report and your correspondence. Frequently, a complaint to the FTC will result in faster action on the part of credit bureaus and check-cashing agencies. Appendix Four contains the addresses of all FTC offices, and sample demand letters to have reinserted fraudulent account data removed from your report can be found in Appendix Four.

If you cannot obtain satisfaction from the credit bureaus with these methods, you might have no alternative but to consider legal action against them. If this is the case, consult an attorney. The law entitles you to damages and penalties, and your paper trail will help your attorney with your case.

The next step to reclaiming your identity is to determine if there are any pending civil actions or judgements against you. This can happen if the identity thieves have rented an apartment in your name and skipped out on the rent, or crossed a creditor who actually will take the time to get a judgment.

If there are, you need to unearth them, because your own wages could be garnisheed to pay off a judgment against an identity thief using your name. You can check at the county courthouse in the counties where the identity thief has been operating. This would include the location where the cards were obtained, and cities where it appears the identity thief has spent some long period of time, based on charges made to the fraudulent accounts. Ask the creditors to send you copies of the statements so you can do your own work.

Many courts will confirm civil judgements over the telephone. If you locate a judgment pending against you, write a letter to the clerk of the court explaining you are a victim of identity theft and that you want the judgment vacated. Enclose a copy of the police report with your letter.

You might be concerned that the identity thief has obtained a drivers license in your name in another state. Based on the pattern of charges, you can send a letter to the relevant state motor vehicle departments notifying them that you have been the victim of identity theft and to check their records for a drivers license obtained in your name. Enclose a copy of the police report. If the state locates a license in your name, they will cancel it and issue an arrest warrant for the person carrying the license. This is one way identity thieves are sometimes caught.

Appendix Four includes sample letters for this purpose, along with a list of addresses for all state motor vehicle departments.

You will also want to make sure that a passport has not been issued in your name. If the identity thief has obtained a passport in your name, the chances are excellent that he will eventually be caught. If the identity thief attempts to re-enter the United States after this fraudulent passport has been invalidated, he will be detained at the port of entry on federal charges.

The U.S. State Department is the agency that issues passports. You should write a letter to them detailing that you are an identity theft victim and any passport issued should be cancelled at once. Enclose the police report with the letter. The address to write to is:

Passport Services
U.S. Department of State
1111 19th Street NW, Suite 500
Washington, DC 20522

The last stop on recovering your good name is to make sure the identity thieves have not made it impossible for you to rent an apartment. Many apartment complex owners obtain tenant screening information from credit bureaus and special companies that record the names and identifiers of those who skip out without paying the rent.

There are hundreds of such firms, and the simplest way to find out if your name is listed is to check to see if any inquiries appear on your credit reports from a service such as these. If so, contact the tenant screening service directly and see if your name shows up in their files. If it does, send them the same type of letter and police report copy that you have to issuers of other fraudulent accounts. Tenant screening services also have a Web site at http://www.n-a-s-a.com, which may contain useful information for you. Once again, if you fail to obtain fast resolution of your problem, send a complaint letter to the FTC and consult a lawyer if all else fails.

Chapter Thirteen
The Internet and Identity Theft

The rapid growth of the Internet, and personal information in cyberspace has made the identity thief's job much easier. Before, hundreds of hardcopy record sources would have to be pored through to develop enough information on a victim before the identity could be stolen. Now it is quite possible, and very easy, for an identity thief located in California to steal the identities of numerous people in Massachusetts, 3,000 miles away. All that is necessary is a computer, a modem, and access to the Internet.

Numerous people locating resources are available at no charge over the Internet. To see how simple it is, we will follow a fictitious scenario of an identity thief located in Seattle who has decided that he wants to steal the identities of upscale professionals located in Pittsburgh, Pennsylvania.

Our villain decides he wants to do the classic identity theft strike. Take over the identity, hit it up for as much financial gain as possible, and then cash out a few months later. He won't get caught and the identity thief can move on to his next victim.

He chooses Pittsburgh because it is far away from his home, and when the scheme finally breaks apart, nothing will exist to connect him thousands of miles away to what happened in Pittsburgh.

He needs to decide on what type of professionals to attack. Our malcontent decides medical doctors are the place to begin. They earn excellent incomes and usually have very good credit profiles once their student loans are repaid.

His first stop will be the American Medical Association's Web site, which features a database of all currently licensed physicians in the United States. The database can be searched by name, location, or specialty. Each physician's entry contains the following information:

- doctor's full name
- specialty
- employer address or practice address
- work telephone number
- medical school attended and year of graduation

This is an excellent start towards acquiring the identifiers necessary to take over a doctor's identity. The next step is to get the doctor's home address and phone number.

A few mouse clicks later the identity thief has access to a choice of Internet databases that contain telephone numbers and addresses. A search here will yield the doctor's home address and telephone number.

The hard work has now been done. The Internet identity thief will then go to an on-line information broker and run a national identifier search to obtain the doctor's Social Security number and birthdate. Once the identity thief has these items, as we have discovered in past chapters, the rest is history.

The Internet allows identity thieves to target victims clear across the country just as easily as if they were targeting a neighbor. Some identity thieves will even target victims in foreign countries. One British identity thief targeted Americans from his home in Manchester, England. After he assembled the necessary data, he flew to the United States, rented inexpensive apartments in his victims' names, and then milked his victims' for as much as possible. A few weeks later he returned to England, $40,000 to $50,000 richer.

Can anything be done to make our identity safer in the age of computers and the Internet? The answer is yes. In the next chapter we will look at some steps that can be taken by government and private industry to make identity theft a crime of the past.

Chapter Fourteen
Stopping Identity Theft

It is not an impossible goal to make identity theft a rare crime. There are a number of simple, straightforward steps that can be taken by both government agencies and private companies to make identity theft very difficult, if not impossible. The reason many of these steps have not been taken is that there are powerful interests who benefit financially from the present arrangement of insecure personal databanks.

We can start with the nation's credit bureaus. We have seen how header information is sold to anyone who is willing to pay the price. This practice needs to be stopped. Congress needs to pass legislation restoring the privacy restrictions on all credit bureau information, not just the account history. This would immediately curtail the problem of identity thieves getting access to victims' Social Security numbers.

Secondly, credit bureaus should be given a fixed date by which they must alter their file-retrieval system so that Social Security numbers are no longer used by the bureau or required by credit applicants. The federal government can provide the industry with appropriations to accomplish this task.

Prescreening should be illegal, unless the consumer has explicitly given his consent. Credit bureaus could send consumers a mailing making their case for prescreening, and let the consumer choose. This is the opposite of the current system where a consumer must explicitly ask to have his name removed from such lists.

All state motor vehicle departments should be prohibited by law from using the Social Security number as the license number, or having it appear on the license document. The license number should also not be derived from the Social Security number.

Any time an individual's driving record is obtained by a third party, the driver concerned should be notified who obtained their driving record. The practice of selling off entire state motor vehicle driver lists should be outlawed.

All private collectors of personal information should have to provide a written warning to the consumer at the time of collection that any personal information provided is subject to resale or trade with other companies unless the consumer checks a box prohibiting such sale or exchange. The laws should impose substantial financial penalties on companies that violate the consumer's wishes.

These simple steps could go a long way toward ending the problem of identity theft. But their enactment would mean that those who profit from the unfettered sale of personal information would lose some lucrative sources of revenue.

Until these laws come to pass, the individual's best hope for avoiding the identity thief is to maintain as low a profile as possible according to the guidelines given previously.

Appendix One
The Federal Trade Commission

The Federal Trade Commission, or FTC for short, regulates the day-to-day operations of credit bureaus, check-clearing services, and tenant screening services. If you are an identity theft victim, and have followed the fight back procedures outlined but are still being hurt by one of these businesses, contact the FTC. Provide copies of all correspondence and a copy of the police report. Their addresses are given below.

FTC Headquarters
Sixth and Pennsylvania Avenue NW
Washington, DC 20580
Phone: (202)-326-2222

FTC
10877 Wilshire Blvd.
Los Angeles, CA 90024
(310) 824-4300

FTC
901 Market Street, #570
San Francisco, CA 94130
(415) 356-5270

FTC
1961 Stout Street, #1523
Denver, CO 80294-0101
(303) 844-2271

FTC
60 Forsyth St. SW, Suite 5M35
Atlanta, GA 30303-2322
(404) 656-1390

FTC
55 East Monroe Street, #1860
Chicago, IL 60603-5701
(312) 960-5633

FTC
101 Merrimac Street, #810
Boston, MA 02114-4719
(617) 424-5960

FTC
150 William Street, #1300
New York, NY 10038
(212) 264-1207

FTC
1111 Superior Avenue #200
Cleveland, OH 44114-2507
(216) 263-3410

FTC
1999 Bryan Street, #2150
Dallas, TX 75201-6808
(214) 979-0213

FTC
2806 Federal Building
915 Second Avenue
Seattle, WA 98174
(206) 220-6350

Appendix Two
What Your Social Security Number Means

The Social Security number plays a key role in identity theft. We have seen that this number allows an identity thief to access quickly many records and files about you. The structure of the Social Security number tells much about its holder. The number can tell where you have lived and your approximate age, among other data.

When the Social Security system was created in the 1930s, the drafters of the system faced a daunting problem of how to come up with a numbering system that would uniquely identify each American, and could grow to accommodate tens of millions of new people as the nation grew in the future.

Each Social Security number would identify the retirement account of one person. People who had the same names and birthdates would need to be positively identified. The nine digit number we know as the Social Security number was created to accomplish this task.

The first three digits of the Social Security number are known as area numbers. Each state and external territory of the United States is assigned one or more of these numbers. For example, Wyoming is assigned the area number 520. New York State, which is much more populous, is assigned the area numbers 050 to 134.

Area numbers are assigned from 001 to 665 and 667 to 699. The area number is determined by which state a person was in when they applied for a Social Security number. If a person obtains a Social Security number shortly after birth, as is now common, this number will reflect the state of birth. If the number was obtained later in life, it will reflect the location of the Social Security office where the applicant applied.

The middle two numbers are called group numbers. These numbers range from 01 to 99. The group numbers can tell a person in what year you got your number. The group number itself does not represent a year, but it can tell how "old"' your Social Security number is.

When assigning Social Security numbers, the government does not simply work through each group in a straight increasing sequence; a convoluted order is followed. The first group numbers used for a given area are the odd numbers below 10, namely 01, 03, 05, 07, and 09. Once these have been assigned the even group numbers 10 to 98 are issued, and after these the even group numbers 02 to 08. The last group numbers issued are the odd group numbers 11 to 99.

The last four digits are known as serial numbers, and these numbers range from 0001 to 9999. Essentially, for any given area and group number, 10,000 different Social Security numbers can be created. The very first Social Security number issued in Wyoming, for example, would have been 520-01-0001. An individual presenting this as his Social Security number had better be close to retirement age.

The last Social Security number that can be issued to someone in Wyoming will be 520-99-9999. When this number has been issued, all of the possible Social Security number combinations that can be issued in the 520 area will be gone. When this happens, this area number is closed, and a new area number will be assigned to this state.

The key point is that an identity thief can use your Social Security number as a way to locate other information about you. If you have an Idaho issued Social Security number, the identity thief may then search Idaho records to learn more about you. This is another reason to avoid giving this number out except when legally necessary.

Appendix Three
Identity Theft Victim Checklist

☐ **Step 1**: Contact all three credit bureaus.

☐ **Step 2**: Send written follow-up letters to credit bureaus.

☐ **Step 3**: Contact local police and file report.

☐ **Step 4**: Contact postal inspectors and file report.

☐ **Step 5**: File fraud report with motor vehicle department, have drivers license number changed.

☐ **Step 6**: Contact all banks and other creditors where fraudulent accounts were opened in writing.

☐ **Step 7**: Contact check-clearing agencies, follow-up letter requesting your name be removed from files.

☐ **Step 8**: Obtain a new Social Security number.

☐ **Step 9**: Check for fraudulently issued passport.

☐ **Step 10**: Check for fraudulently obtained judgments in your name, send letter to court for removal.

☐ **Step 11**: Check for criminal records in your name, write to relevant agency to start removal process.

Appendix Four
Letters, Forms and Information

On the following pages appear sample letters that an identity theft victim may need to write to banks, credit bureaus, and other agencies. Use these as a model, making sure to include all of the necessary information including your name, address, birthdate, and Social Security number (only if necessary). You'll also find a copy of Form W-7 (Application for IRS Individual Taxpayer Identification Number) and a list of useful addresses. All correspondence should be photocopied and sent certified mail, return receipt requested. A well-documented paper trail is very valuable should it become necessary for you to take legal action against a bank or credit bureau.

Letter to Credit Bureau After
First Telephone Call

Date

Your name
Your Social Security number
Your birthdate
Your full address

To Whom It May Concern:

Following my conversation on (date), with (representative name), I was assured you would remove the following fraudulent accounts from my credit report and place a fraud block on same. Please send me a copy of my corrected report as soon as possible.

Fraudulent accounts:

Thank You,

Signature

Letter to Credit Bureau if Inaccurate Data Reappears

Date

Your name
Your Social Security number
Your birthdate
Your full address

To Whom It May Concern:

Following my conversation with (representative name) on (date), I was assured that the following fraudulent accounts would be deleted from my credit report. These accounts still appear on my credit report. If you do not delete these accounts at once, I will be forced to file a dispute with the Federal Trade Commission. I am a victim of identity theft, and a copy of the police report is enclosed.

Fraudulent accounts:

Thank You,

Signature

Letter to Creditor Where Fraudulent Account has been opened

Date

Your name
Your address

To Whom It May Concern:

The following account (account number and details), was opened in my name by an identity thief. Please close this account at once and stop reporting it to the credit bureau in my name. Enclosed is a copy of the police report.

Thank you,

Signature

First Letter to Check-Clearing Agency

Date

Your name
Your address

To Whom It May Concern:

The following account was opened fraudulently in my name by an identity thief: (account details). Please remove my name, drivers license number and Social Security number from your database. Enclosed is a copy of the police report documenting the theft of my identity.

Thank you,

Signature

Second Letter to Check-Clearing Service

Date

Your name
Your address

To Whom It May Concern:

I contacted you on (date), asking that my name, drivers license number and Social Security number be removed from your database. I am a victim of identity theft, and a copy of the police report is again enclosed. If you do not remove my identifiers from your files I will be forced to file a dispute with the Federal Trade Commission.

Thank you,

Signature

Letter to Court Clerk Requesting Removal of Judgment

Date

Your name
Your address

To Whom It May Concern:

The following civil judgments were obtained in my name by an identity thief: (judgment names/references). Enclosed is a copy of the police report documenting the theft of my identity. Please expunge these judgments at once, as they are harming me.

Thank you,

Signature

Letter to Out of State Motor Vehicle Department

Date

Your name
Your address

To Whom It May Concern:

   I am a victim of identity theft and am worried that the identity thief may have obtained a fraudulent drivers license in my name in your state. Enclosed is a copy of the police report documenting the theft of my identity. Please search your records for any such license, cancel it at once, and notify me of your results.

Thank you,

Signature

Letter to State Department Passport Office

Date

Your name
Your address

To Whom It May Concern:

I am the victim of identity theft and am worried that the thief may have obtained a fraudulent passport in my name. Enclosed is a copy of the police report documenting the theft of my identity. Please cancel any passport issued and notify me of the results of your search.

Thank you,

Signature

Letter to Internal Revenue Service

Date

Your name
Your address

Dear Sir:

I am the victim of an identity thief and the thief may have earned income and reportable interest under my name and Social Security number. Enclosed is a copy of the police report documenting the theft of my identity. Please send me all records of any interest or income that are not shown on the enclosed documentation.

Thank you,

Signature

Letter to District Attorney or Police Agency

Date

Your name
Your address

Dear Sir:

I am the victim of identity theft. A conviction was made against me by your agency (case details). Enclosed is a copy of the police report documenting the theft of my identity. I need to know what steps I must take to have my name and identifiers removed from this conviction record, as it was obtained by the identity thief using my name.

Thank you,

Signature

The following companies provide various identity documents, which could be useful to identity thieves:

ID World
4038 NW 9th Avenue
Oakland Park, FL 33309

Photo ID Systems
831 Granville Street
Vancouver, BC V6Z 1K7
Canada

Couch Potato Publishing
4211 Little Road, Suite 9
New Port Richey, FL 34655

Specialty Document Company
P.O. Box 5684
El Monte, CA 91731

Maxsell Corporation
P.O. Box 23021
Fort Lauderdale, FL 33307

NIC, Inc.
P.O. Box 5950
Shreveport, LA 71135

Ideal Studios
P.O. Box 41156
Chicago, IL 60641

Form **W-7** (Rev. February 1998) Department of the Treasury Internal Revenue Service	**Application for IRS Individual Taxpayer Identification Number** ▶ See instructions. ▶ Please type or print. ▶ For use by individuals who are NOT U.S. citizens, nationals, or permanent residents.	OMB No. 1545-1483

Please note the following when completing this form:
- This number is for tax purposes only. **Do not submit** this form if you have, or are eligible to obtain, a U.S. social security number (SSN).
- Receipt of an ITIN creates no inference regarding your immigration status or your right to work in the United States.
- Receipt of an ITIN does not make you eligible to claim the earned income credit (EIC).

FOR IRS USE ONLY

Reason you are submitting Form W-7. (Check only one box. See instructions.)
- a ☐ Nonresident alien required to obtain ITIN to claim tax treaty benefit
- b ☐ Nonresident alien filing a U.S. tax return and not eligible for an SSN
- c ☐ U.S. resident alien (based on days present in the United States) filing a U.S. tax return and not eligible for an SSN
- d ☐ Dependent of U.S. person ⎫ Enter name and SSN of U.S. person (see instructions) ▶ ....
- e ☐ Spouse of U.S. person ⎭ ....
- f ☐ Other (specify) ....

1 Name (see instructions)
Name at birth if different ▶

	1a Last name (surname or family name)	First name	Middle name
	1b Last name (surname or family name)	First name	Middle name

2 Permanent residence address, if any (see instructions)

Street address, apartment number, or rural route number. Do not use a P.O. box number.

City or town, state or province, and country. Include ZIP code or postal code where appropriate.

3 Mailing address (if different from above)

Street address, apartment number, P.O. box number, or rural route number.

City or town, state or province, and country. Include ZIP code or postal code where appropriate.

4 Birth information

Date of birth (month, day, year) / /	Country of birth	City and state or province (optional)	**5** ☐ Male ☐ Female

6 Family information (see instructions)

Father's last name (surname)	First name	Middle name
Mother's maiden name (surname)	First name	Middle name

7 Other information

7a Country(ies) of citizenship	7b Foreign tax identification number	7c Type of U.S. visa (if any) and expiration date

7d Describe identification document(s) submitted (see instructions).
☐ Passport ☐ Driver's license/State I.D. ☐ INS documentation ☐ Other....................
Issued by: Number:

7e Have you previously received a U.S. temporary Taxpayer Identification Number (TIN) or Employer Identification Number (EIN)?
☐ No/Do not know. Skip line 7f.
☐ Yes. Complete line 7f. If you need more space, list on a sheet and attach to this form. (See instructions.)

7f TIN ☐☐☐-☐☐-☐☐☐☐   EIN ☐☐-☐☐☐☐☐☐☐
Enter the name under which the TIN was issued.   Enter the name under which the EIN was issued.

Sign Here

Under penalties of perjury, I (applicant/delegate/acceptance agent) declare that I have examined this application, including accompanying documentation and statements, and to the best of my knowledge and belief, it is true, correct, and complete. I authorize the IRS to disclose to my acceptance agent returns or return information necessary to resolve matters regarding the assignment of my IRS individual taxpayer identification number (ITIN).

Signature of applicant (if delegate, see instructions) ▶	Date (month, day, year) / /	Phone number

Keep a copy of this form for your records.

Name of delegate, if applicable (type or print) ▶	Delegate's relationship to applicant	☐ Parent ☐ Guardian

Acceptance Agent's Use ONLY

Signature ▶	Date (month, day, year) / /	Phone: ( ) FAX: ( )
Name and title (type or print) ▶	Name of company	EIN

For Paperwork Reduction Act Notice, see page 4.   Cat. No. 10229L   Form **W-7** (Rev. 2-98)

Identity Theft
The Cybercrime of the Millennium

96

Form W-7 (Rev. 2-98)

General Instructions

Note: *If you have been lawfully admitted for permanent residence or U.S. employment, you are eligible for a social security number. Do not complete this form.*

Purpose of Form

Use Form W-7 to apply for an IRS individual taxpayer identification number (ITIN). An ITIN is a nine-digit number issued by the U.S. Internal Revenue Service (IRS) to individuals who are required to have a U.S. taxpayer identification number but who do not have, and are not eligible to obtain, a social security number (SSN).

The ITIN is for tax purposes only. It does not entitle you to Social Security benefits, and creates no inference regarding your immigration status or your right to work in the United States. Any individual who is eligible to be legally employed in the United States must have an SSN.

Note: *Individuals filing tax returns using an ITIN are not eligible for the earned income credit (EIC).*

Who Must Apply

Any individual who is **not eligible to obtain an SSN** but who must furnish a taxpayer identification number to the IRS must apply for an ITIN on Form W-7. For example:

● A nonresident alien individual not eligible for an SSN who is required to file a U.S. tax return OR who is filing a U.S. tax return only to claim a refund.

● A nonresident alien individual not eligible for an SSN who elects to file a joint U.S. tax return with a spouse who is a U.S. citizen or resident.

● A U.S. resident alien (based on substantial presence) who files a U.S. tax return but who is not eligible for an SSN.

● An alien spouse claimed as an exemption on a U.S. tax return who is not eligible to obtain an SSN.

● An alien individual eligible to be claimed as a dependent on a U.S. tax return but who is unable or not eligible to obtain an SSN.

DO NOT complete Form W-7 if you have an SSN **or** you are eligible to obtain an SSN. Thus, do not complete this form if you are a U.S. citizen or national, or if you have been lawfully admitted for permanent residence or U.S. employment.

To obtain an SSN, use **Form SS-5,** Application for a Social Security Card. To get Form SS-5 or to find out if you are eligible to obtain an SSN, contact a Social Security Administration office.

If you have an application for an SSN pending, **do not** file Form W-7. Complete Form W-7 only if the Social Security Administration notifies you that an SSN cannot be issued.

Additional Information

Publications. For details on resident and nonresident alien status and the tests for residence (including the substantial presence test), get **Pub. 519,** U.S. Tax Guide for Aliens.

For details on individuals who can be claimed as dependents and on obtaining an SSN for a dependent, get **Pub. 501,** Exemptions, Standard Deduction, and Filing Information.

For details on eligibility for the earned income credit, get **Pub. 596,** Earned Income Credit.

These publications are available free from the IRS. To order the publications, call 1-800-TAX-FORM (1-800-829-3676) if you are in the United States. If you have a foreign address, you can write to either:

● Eastern Area Distribution Center
P.O. Box 25866
Richmond, VA 23286-8107

OR

● Western Area Distribution Center
Rancho Cordova, CA 95743-0001

You can also get these publications using a computer and modem. You can use:

● Internet:
World Wide Web: Connect to www.irs.ustreas.gov
File transfer protocol services: Connect to ftp.irs.ustreas.gov.
Telnet to iris.irs.telnet.gov.

● Internal Revenue Information Services (IRIS) on FedWorld, a government bulletin board. IRIS is accessible directly using your modem by calling 703-321-8020.

Telephone help. If, after reading these instructions and our free publications, you are not sure how to complete your application or have additional questions, you may call for assistance:

● Inside the United States: 1-800-829-1040, Monday through Saturday from 7:00 a.m. to 11:00 p.m. (in Alaska from 6:00 a.m. to 10:00 p.m. and in Hawaii from 5:00 a.m. to 9:00 p.m.)

● Outside the United States: 1-215-516-ITIN (215-516-4846). This is not a toll-free number. You may also contact any of our overseas offices in Bonn, London, Mexico City, Paris, Rome, Santiago, Singapore, Sydney, or Tokyo.

How To Apply

You can apply either by mail or in person. See **Where To Apply** on this page. Keep a copy for your records. Be sure to mail or bring with you:

● Your completed Form W-7; and

● The original documents, or certified or notarized copies of documents, that substantiate the information provided on the Form W-7.

The document(s) you present must be current and must verify: **(a)** your identity, that is, contain your name and a photograph, and **(b)** support your claim of foreign status. You may have to provide a combination of documents for this purpose. Examples of acceptable documents include, but are not limited to:

● A passport.

● A driver's license.

● Documents issued by the U.S. Immigration and Naturalization Service (INS).

● An identity card issued by a state or national government authority.

● A foreign military or military dependent identification card.

● A foreign voter registration certificate.

● Birth, marriage, or baptismal certificates.

● School records.

You can submit copies of original documents. However, such documents must be

● Certified by the issuing agency or official custodian of the original record; or

● Notarized by a U.S. notary public legally authorized within his or her local jurisdiction to certify that the document is a true copy of the original. U.S. notaries public are available at U.S. embassies and consulates worldwide. Non-U.S. notarizations will **not** be accepted.

When To Apply

Complete Form W-7 as soon as you meet one of the requirements listed under **Who Must Apply** on this page. Applying early will give the IRS time to issue you an ITIN before its required use.

If you have not heard from the IRS regarding your ITIN within 30 days, you may call 1-800-829-1040 (in the United States) or 1-215-516-4846 (outside the United States) to find out about the status of your application. Be sure to have a copy of your application available when you call. Please allow 30 days from the date you submitted Form W-7 before calling the IRS about the status of your application.

Allow 4 to 6 weeks for the IRS to notify you in writing of your ITIN.

Where To Apply

Applying in person. You can apply for an ITIN at any IRS walk-in office in the United States and at most IRS offices abroad (contact the IRS office abroad to find out if that office accepts Form W-7 applications). You can also get application forms at certain U.S. consular offices.

You can also apply through an acceptance agent authorized by the IRS.

Applying by mail. Complete Form W-7, sign and date it, and mail the form along with the original or certified or notarized copies of your documentation to:

Internal Revenue Service
Philadelphia Service Center
ITIN Unit
P.O. Box 447
Bensalem, PA 19020

Original documents you submit will be returned to you. You do not need to provide a return envelope. Copies of documents will not be returned.

Specific Instructions

The following instructions are for those items that are not self-explanatory. Enter N/A (not applicable) on all lines that do not apply. If you are completing this form for someone else, answer the questions as they apply to that person.

Reason for applying. You must check a box to indicate the reason you are completing this Form W-7. **Check only one box.**

a. Nonresident alien required to obtain ITIN to claim tax treaty benefit. Certain

Form W-7 (Rev. 2-98)

nonresident aliens must obtain an ITIN to claim a tax treaty benefit even if they do not have to file a U.S. tax return.

b. Nonresident alien filing a U.S. tax return and not eligible for an SSN. This category includes:

● A nonresident alien who must file a U.S. tax return to report income effectively or not effectively connected with the conduct of a trade or business in the United States.

● A nonresident alien who is filing a U.S. tax return only to obtain a refund.

● A nonresident alien electing to file a U.S. tax return jointly with a spouse who is a U.S. citizen or resident.

c. U.S. resident alien (based on days present in the United States) filing a U.S. tax return and not eligible for an SSN. A foreign individual living in the United States who does not have permission to work from the INS, and is thus ineligible for an SSN, may still have a U.S. tax return filing obligation. Such individuals must check this box.

d. Dependent of U.S. person. This is an individual who may be claimed as a dependent on a U.S. tax return and who is unable, or not eligible, to obtain an SSN.

Note: *A U.S. person is a citizen, national, or resident alien of the United States.*

e. Spouse of U.S. person. This is a nonresident alien husband or wife who is not filing a U.S. tax return (including a joint return) but who may be claimed as a spouse for an exemption, and who is not eligible to obtain an SSN.

f. Other. Use this box only if your situation does not fall into any of the above categories. If you check this box, you must describe in detail your reason for requesting an ITIN.

SSN of U.S. person. If you are applying for an ITIN under category d or e above, you **must** provide the **full name and SSN** of the U.S. person. Enter the information in the space provided. If the U.S. person chooses to provide this information in a separate letter, be sure to enter "Information will be provided in separate letter" in this space. If this space is left blank, your application will be rejected.

The letter provided by the U.S. person must identify the Form W-7 to which the information relates and must include:

● The U.S. person's full name and SSN; **and**

● The name, address, date of birth and country of birth of the dependent or spouse as shown on the Form W-7.

Mail the letter to the address shown under **Where To Apply** on page 3.

Note: *If the U.S. person chooses this method, the Form W-7 will not be processed until the information is received.*

Lines 1a and 1b. Enter your legal name on line 1a. This entry should reflect your name as it will appear on your U.S. tax return. If your legal name was different at birth, enter on line 1b your name at birth as it appears on your birth certificate.

Line 2. Enter your complete address in the country where you permanently or normally reside. If you are claiming a benefit under an income tax treaty with the United States, the address entered must normally be an address in the treaty country. Include the postal code where appropriate.

Do not use a Post Office box or an "in care of" (c/o) address instead of a street address. It will not be accepted.

Line 3. Enter your mailing address if it is different from the address on line 2. This is the address the IRS will use to mail you written notification of your ITIN.

Line 4. You **must** identify the country in which you were born.

Line 7b. If your country of residence for tax purposes has issued you a tax identification number, enter that number on line 7b. For example, if you are a resident of Canada, you would enter your Canadian Social Insurance Number.

Line 7c. Enter only U.S. nonimmigrant visa information, for example, "B-1/B-2." Also enter the expiration date of the visa.

Line 7d. If you have a passport, use it to provide verification of your identity and foreign status. Check the "Passport" box.

If you do not have a passport, use a driver's license or official identification card issued by a U.S. or foreign governmental jurisdiction and check the appropriate box.

If you are using documents issued by the INS, check the "INS documentation" box.

If you have none of the above, check the box for "Other" and **specifically identify** the type(s) of document you are using (for example, "military ID" for a military or military/dependent identification card). You may have to provide more than one current document to verify your identity and foreign status. At least one document you present should contain a recent photograph.

You must provide the name of the state, country, or other issuer, and the identification number (if any) appearing on the document(s) you provide. You may be required to provide a translation of documents in a foreign language.

Line 7e.—If you ever received a "temporary Taxpayer Identification Number" (TIN) or an Employer Identification Number (EIN), check the "Yes" box and enter the number on line 7f. If you never had a temporary TIN or an EIN, or you do not know your temporary TIN, check the "No/Do not know" box.

A "temporary TIN" was a nine-digit number issued by the IRS to individuals before 1996. You would have been issued this number if you filed a U.S. tax return and did not have a social security number. This temporary TIN will appear on any correspondence the IRS sent you concerning that return. You may have been issued more than one temporary TIN. If so, attach a separate sheet listing all the temporary TINs you received.

An EIN is a nine-digit number assigned by the IRS to businesses, such as sole proprietorships.

Line 7g. Enter in the space provided the temporary TIN and/or EIN and the name under which the number was issued.

Signature. Generally, Form W-7 **must be signed by the applicant.** However, if the applicant is a minor 14 years of age or younger, a delegate (parent or guardian) should sign for him or her. Type or print the delegate's name in the space provided and check the appropriate box to indicate the relationship to the applicant.

If the applicant is over 14 years of age but unable or legally incompetent to sign, the applicant may appoint an authorized agent to sign. The authorized agent must print his or her name in the space provided for the name of the delegate and must attach **Form 2848,** Power of Attorney and Declaration of Representative.

Paperwork Reduction Act Notice. We ask for the information on this form to carry out the Internal Revenue laws of the United States. You are required to give us the information. We need it to ensure that you are complying with these laws and to allow us to figure and collect the right amount of tax.

You are not required to provide the information requested on a form that is subject to the Paperwork Reduction Act unless the form displays a valid OMB control number. Books or records relating to a form or its instructions must be retained as long as their contents may become material in the administration of any Internal Revenue law. Generally, tax returns and return information are confidential, as required by Internal Revenue Code section 6103.

The time needed to complete and file this form will vary depending on individual circumstances. The estimated average time is: **Learning about the law or the form,** 13 min.; **Preparing the form,** 29 min.; **Copying, assembling, and sending the form to the IRS,** 20 min.

If you have comments concerning the accuracy of these time estimates or suggestions for making this form simpler, we would be happy to hear from you. You can write to the Tax Forms Committee, Western Area Distribution Center, Rancho Cordova, CA 95743-0001. **DO NOT** send the form to this address. Instead, see **Where To Apply** on page 3.

YOU WILL ALSO WANT TO READ: